The Ecstasies of St. Francis

The Ecstasies of St. Francis

JOHN RYAN HAULE

LINDISFARNE BOOKS

© 2004 by John Ryan Haule

Published by Lindisfarne Books
400 Main Street
Great Barrington, MA 01230
www.lindisfarne.org

Library of Congress Cataloging-in-Publication data

Haule, John R., 1942-
The ecstasies of St. Francis : the way of lady poverty / John Ryan
Haule. — 1st. ed.
p. cm.
Includes bibliographical references.
ISBN 1-58420-010-3
1. Francis, of Assisi, Saint, 1182-1226. 2. Christian
saints — Italy — Assisi — Biography. 3. Spiritual life — Catholic Church.
I. Title: Ecstasies of St. Francis. II. Title
BX4700.F6H35 2003
271'.302—dc22
2003020150

10 9 8 7 6 5 4 3 2 1

Printed in the United States of America
by The P.A. Hutchison Company.

100% post-consumer waste paper

For Robert,

The Yellow Sea of whose
Soulscape
Corroded
The features of everyday,
Freeing betimes
The Winged Ones
Most of us
Fail to see.

In memoriam
April 13, 1948–August 8, 1993

CONTENTS

~

A Note on the Early Biographies

THE EARLY BIOGRAPHIES of St. Francis of Assisi (1181–1226) have been assembled in *St. Francis of Assisi, Writings and Early Biographies: English Omnibus of the Sources for the Life of St. Francis,* edited by Marion A. Habig (1983). The individual "legends" (i.e., "biographies designed to be read aloud") that the *Omnibus* contains are listed below in the order of their probable dates of composition. Roman numerals in the references refer to chapter titles, Arabic numerals to paragraph numbers. Thus (*MajLife*: II, 5) designates Chapter Two, paragraph 5, of Bonaventure's *Major Life.*

LadyP

(1227) *Sacrum Commercium* [*The Holy Intercourse of Francis and His Lady Poverty*]: a classic work of religious allegory written by an unknown friar in the year following Francis's death.

1Celano

(1228) *First Life of St. Francis* written by Friar Thomas of Celano for the solemn ceremony of the saint's canonization.

2Celano

(1245) *Second Life of St. Francis* written by Thomas of Celano, including anecdotes that came to light after the writing of *1Celano* and retelling some old events with new emphases.

L3Comps
(1246) *The Legend of the Three Companions*: the recollections of three of Francis's closest early companions, Bros. Leo, Angelo, and Rufino, edited by Bro. Angelo.

Perugia
(1246) *The Legend of Perugia*: scrolls found in Perugia in 1311 that are generally agreed to have been assembled by Bro. Leo, companion, secretary, nurse, and confessor of St. Francis.

3Celano
(1250) *Third Life of St. Francis* written by Thomas of Celano, mostly a compilation of the miracles attributed to Francis.

MajLife
(1263) *Major Life of St. Francis* written by St. Bonaventure when he was Minister General of the Order of Friars Minor. Because the material in the available biographies was fueling arguments over the identity of the Franciscan Order, Bonaventure was asked to produce an "official biography" in a spirit of peace and reconciliation. In 1266, all earlier biographies were ordered destroyed; and friars everywhere complied with this order. We possess them today only because non-Franciscan monasteries had copies they felt under no obligation to destroy.

MinLife
(1266) *Minor Life of St. Francis* written by Bonaventure to be included in recitation of the Divine Office during the eight days following the feast of St. Francis on October 4.

Mirror
(1318) *The Mirror of Perfection*: a collection of anecdotes with special emphasis on traditions ignored by Bonaventure. The unknown editor opposed monastic regulations that had crept into the Order.

Flowers
(1340) *The Little Flowers of St. Francis*: the most widely read life, written by an unknown Italian Friar.

ONE

Rearranging Our Sensibilities

THE IMPETUS FOR this book was a powerful piece of music, Olivier Messiaen's opera, *Saint François d'Assise*. Before Messiaen rearranged my sensibilities, I had paid scant attention to the little man in robe and tonsure who is remembered primarily for preaching to the birds. He seemed too much a child, too simple-minded, too pious—out of touch with the harsher realities of life. In fact, when I told my brother I had been reading thirteenth and fourteenth century biographies of the saint, he remembered one of the nuns who taught in our grade school nearly a half century ago saying that St. Francis was a "sissy." Perhaps his memory is faulty. Perhaps the nun was commenting on the pronunciation of Assisi. However flawed the story, though, it is memorable for expressing a common opinion in a shocking manner. Possibly we think it was permissible for Francis to have been a sissy, for he loved God enough to become a "saint." Or perhaps all saints are sissies to some extent. Such notions lodge in our minds unexamined and reinforce the distance we habitually maintain between "the real world" and religious aspiration.

The Francis of Messiaen's opera is a bird of a different feather. First performed in Paris in 1983, the opera employs all the idiosyncratic forces of Messiaen's craft, especially the extraordinary "colors" of his unusual chord structures ("modes") and melodies derived from his life-long study of bird song. Messiaen (1908–1992) was a conservative Roman Catholic who considered himself a mystic and composed "liturgies" for organ, as well as the better-known *Quartet for the End of Time*, which was written during World War II while he was a captive of the Nazis. Messiaen set out to give us the inner life of St. Francis and did so by selecting a few well-known scenes from the earliest biographies and investing them with an emotional reality that only music can convey. There is nothing sentimental, effeminate, childish, or superficial about this Francis. The music is almost disturbing. Composed of melodic fragments drawn from the songs of specific European and tropical birds, it creates a sensibility that transcends the merely human and gives us something larger, impersonal, almost cosmic. Dark conflict and discord struggle with sweetness and light in the soul of a hero—neither naïve nor jaded—who has surpassed us not so much by his goodness as by the depth of his struggle. Here, for the first time, was an interesting Francis, one who might have something to say to us today.

To find the evidence for this other Francis, I acquired a copy of the nearly 2000–page *Omnibus of Sources* containing the many versions of his life (Habig, 1983). Here, despite differences between biographies, I found an original and uncompromising character, one who seemed to belong in the pages of my earlier, still unpublished study of Tantra. Not that Francis is a "sexual mystic"—though his relationship with Lady Poverty has distinct erotic overtones. Rather Francis resembles the *tantrikas*, the practitioners of Tantra, in that he has taken up the shadow side of his existence, the most disturbing experiences in life, and pursued them relentlessly as the means to achieve higher states of consciousness—"ecstasies," in which one "stands outside" (*ek-stasis*) one's ordinary self and outside the everyday world in order to contemplate and to live a larger reality. Like the more disreputable saints of Tantra, Francis sought out experiences that scared, disgusted, aroused, and humiliated, while cultivating equanimity in the face of them. He found social conformity to be a distraction that would dull his sensitivity to the other-worldly dimensions of life and so he deliberately courted public scorn and rejection. In contrast to the world of public consensus, Francis discovered an alternate cosmos, a sacred world, which he recognized as the "kingdom of God" that Jesus had come to preach—not a life after death but an alternate and supremely meaningful way to live right here in one's temporal body-and-mind. The kingdom of God was a way of *seeing* the world, a state of consciousness that might fade in and out but that Francis hoped to learn how to stabilize.

Francis, therefore, set out to change his consciousness, and he began precisely where the tantrikas began, with his own body-and-mind. By monitoring his mental and physiological states, he paid attention to what happened to his awareness when life presented him with a challenge or an opportunity. The action he took in response to such events brought about another change in consciousness, and he noted that as well. He did not need to flee the world like a hermit in order to stay in a cosmos of bliss. He threw himself into the world of poverty and sorrow, caring for lepers, rebuilding churches, preaching sermons, begging for his bread. But he did these things mindfully, and did not lose sight of the fact that the real field of his labors lay within.

Paradoxically, Francis did change the world. He began a reform within the church, revealed a new emotional sort of spirituality, and inspired thousands to follow his lead. But that is not the Francis who gripped me. I am drawn to the one who learned to experiment with his own awareness. If we can figure out how an innovator like this operates, then perhaps we can learn to re-enchant the world for ourselves. Francis's predilection was for the practice of poverty, a carefully observed set of spiritual exercises that only apparently makes pennilessness and ragged clothes the center of one's life. As we will see, his attention to what these practices did to his awareness is the chief thing, the essence of his spiritual practice. To emphasize the disciplined spiritual practice that poverty became for Francis, I shall refer to it with the Sanskrit term *sadhana* ("spiritual practice"). The sadhana of poverty, then, is not simply a matter of giving up luxuries but rather the mindfulness with which poverty is practiced.

We can learn from Francis even if our own predilection is not the pursuit of poverty. Any field of activity conscientiously engaged in with the sort of mindfulness that highlights the changes in our consciousness may become a sadhana whereby the world is transformed for us, and ourselves along with it. Possibly we will not want to call this alternate universe the "kingdom of God." We may leave such determinations to each individual's own "theological"—or "cosmic" or "psychological"—proclivities. The point is that in working with his body-and-mind Francis employs his own "human nature" to accomplish the spiritual transformation that has made him the saint we have remembered these past eight centuries. We, too, have a human nature. Our body-and-mind goes wherever we go. Francis has exemplified how we may use our standard-issue humanity to make life transcendently meaningful.

In the chapters that follow, we shall examine the life of Francis as told by his earliest biographers, for it was their intention to convey the spiritual attitude Francis passed on to his disciples. A glance at "A Note on the Early Biographies" (on the page following the Table of Contents) shows that these documents are of three sorts. Some appear to be personal testimonies written by Francis's closest followers. Others were commissioned by the church or the Franciscan Order to support the official view of Francis. The third group was composed by Franciscan enthusiasts who lived too long after the events they describe to have been witnesses to anything but the popular memory of Francis. There is no "objective," historically accurate picture of the saint, but there is a great deal of agreement among the several portraits that remain.

In Chapter Two, we shall consider in general terms the difference between Franciscan and Catholic propaganda and the unexpunged evidence that Francis saw himself differently from the way he is officially portrayed. Our job will be to pay attention less to reports of the miraculous than to what Francis was doing with his consciousness. In Chapter Three, we shall investigate the sadhana of poverty, and see how he strove for "perfect joy," the emotion that ratified the appearance of the sacred cosmos, and distinguished it from lesser enjoyments. We shall notice that he also paid attention to feelings of shame and evaluated the message they were giving him about the purity or impurity of his intentions. Then, in Chapter Four, we shall take up his love affair with Lady Poverty and note its parallels in his relationships with Clare, the founder of the Franciscan sisterhood, and Jacoba, his friend and benefactress. Thus we shall come to see that the sadhana of poverty is an erotic undertaking. Eros describes the emotion and physiology of arousal and its transformation of the conscious field. The fact that it was central to Francis's practice implies no compromise with his celibacy. It describes, rather, his longing—the fact that divine union and the final and complete establishment of the sacred cosmos are always goals to be eagerly approached, like union with the beloved.

Having thereby described the foundation of his daily practice, in Chapter Five we shall look at Francis's growth in prayer or meditation and the ecstatic states he achieved. His was a cosmic mysticism, not merely a vision to be glimpsed but a cosmos in which to participate actively, knowingly, and with joy. The remarkable events that occurred when he was joyfully participating in the sacred cosmos have been presented as miracles by the medieval biographers. As we shall see, however, many of them belong to the category of phenomena that the Hindus call *siddhis*, the "special powers" that come naturally when one is in high-level ecstatic states of consciousness (Chapter Six).

Although we have no texts of his sermons, we have many accounts of his style of preaching. Often it involved gestures and dramatic gambits even more than words. His preaching exemplifies perhaps better than any other activity his experimental, ecstatic style. He employed a kind of spontaneous improvisation to get across his vision and change the consciousness of his listeners (Chapter Seven).

In Chapter Eight we shall examine how Francis brought everything he had learned from his sadhana and his ecstasies to everyday life with his brother friars. The best examples of this come from memories of his closest companions, written down after Francis's death— how they lived together in paradisal joy and love in those early days when they inhabited an abandoned building on the bank of the Rivo Torto (Tortuous River). They followed as serpentine a path as that river, winding from epiphany to epiphany, as the entire world glowed with sacred, inner light.

In Chapter Nine, we shall examine the last crisis of Francis's life: as he saw it, the final demand that God made on him, to accept the ecclesiastical veil that was being thrown over his religious order. The sadhana of religious poverty was no longer to be followed; the paradisal life he and his followers had lived by the Rivo Torto was forever a thing of the past. In challenging everything he had stood for, the crisis made possible the final apotheosis, the ultimate ecstasy, and a new manifestation of the sacred cosmos. The hagiographers allude to this transformation when they describe his vision of the crucified Seraph, and the appearance of his stigmata.

In the final chapter, we shall look back over Francis's achievements and propose a variant program to the sadhana of poverty that a modern individual might follow.

TWO

Loosening the Veil Around Francis

As soon as he reached the bishop's presence, he made no
delay, he never hesitated for a moment, or said or listened to
a word from anyone; instead, he tore off all his clothes,
including even his trousers, and stood there naked before
them all. He seemed to be beside himself in his fervor, and he
was not ashamed to be stripped naked for love of Christ who
hung naked for us all on the Cross (*MinLife*: I, 7).

BEHIND THE BROWN-robed little man earnestly instructing birds,
lies a life of disciplined experimentation. Because Francis of Assisi
fasted and forswore any sort of ownership, even the clothes on his
back, we tend to think he was heroically self-depriving. Why else
would a man resolve to live on what he could beg from the patrons at
his local fast-food joint, and give his car to a man found limping along
the highway? We think of self-flagellation, of "sacrifices" to win God's
favor or to compensate for our guilt. For us, self-denial is grim business, a way to earn chips in a cheerless present that can be cashed out
in some ghostly future erected by faith. We think you have to have a
blind and naïve conviction devoid of evidence to live in the world of

space and time as though *it* were the phantom and life after death the incontrovertible reality. When we think this way, we construct a Francis who might have lived in *our* world. Our assumptions about life, death, and religious conviction weave a veil that hides the radically different universe Francis actually inhabited and prevents us from knowing who he was.

Every mystic lives in a radically different world than the one we take for granted. Francis saw the same sorts of objects and events we see. He just organized them differently. Or—more accurately said— he *discovered* the world to have a different organization and to require a different sort of response than the world inhabited by the rest of us. His bodily and mental experimentation altered his consciousness so that the world of everyday dissolved into a sacred universe: God's world, the kingdom of heaven, the land- and mindscape revealed by Jesus. No little calculation and learning from experience went into his daily spiritual exercises. Francis was a savvy, determined, and one-pointed man: not unlike his father, the textile trader. Both of them improvised daring moves, studied the play of their competitors, learned from their mistakes, and capitalized on their profits. It takes as tough a mind to be a mystic as it does to make a fortune in the business world. Pietro di Barnardone and his son Francesco approached life in a similar manner, though they lived in disparate universes.

Father and Son

As the shaman drums, dances, or drugs his way into a trance that opens his eyes to an alternate world, as real in its own way as a Friday night rush hour, so Francis's daily practices maintained a sacred and alternate cosmos in which things looked and felt different than they do to us. Sometimes he did dance, and he sang a great deal. But unlike the shaman, he did not employ these activities as "techniques of ecstasy," devices to move him out of the everyday world into the sacred cosmos. In Francis's case, he sang and danced because he was *already* there, filled with enthusiasm and joy as he looked about and saw that the world and everything in it represented an outpouring of divine generosity. It was thrilling to be part of it all—brother to the birds, the streams, the sun and sky, the beggars and lepers.

His father was proud to have made himself into a "major citizen," one of the *maiores* in the town of Assisi, by dint of his cleverness and hard work. He had set his son up to rise still further, to become a knight and therefore a "gentleman" if he so chose. Francis went the other way. He aspired to be a "minor citizen," like the poor, God's humblest children, and insisted that he and his disciples be known as Friars Minor, *fratres minores*.

Francis's primary "technique of ecstasy" was his practice of poverty. On the one hand it amounted to a systematic reversal of everything his father stood for; and since his father was a remarkably successful merchant, Francis's inversion constituted a repudiation of the profane world in precisely that sector in which it was most successful. The foundations of modern capitalism were being laid very effectively by Pietro di Bernardone and his cohorts[1]; feudalism was failing; and the nobility was beginning a decline which would become evident in the next two centuries. Francis seized upon the central premise of capitalism, acquisition and financial leverage, and turned it inside out. He became a dedicated spendthrift. Everything that fell into his hands by humble labor, begging, or the spontaneous generosity of his admirers he gave away at his earliest opportunity. His competitors were not the upwardly mobile but society's outcasts and downtrodden. If he found a beggar whose clothes were more worn out and patched than his own, he offered an exchange. He traded downward as resolutely as his father traded upward.

For Francis, no dependable security was to be found in clothing, shelter, money in the bank, or the praise of his contemporaries. These were the things that might have kept him in the kingdom of this world and shut off his access to the kingdom of heaven. He strove to depend without reserve on the providence of a God who clothes the lilies of the fields and the birds of the air more gloriously than Solomon. Freespending poverty was his spiritual practice, his technique of ecstasy. Every move in the strategy of poverty removed another stone from the foundation of the profane world and firmed up the spiritual undergirding of the sacred cosmos.

Although he looked to the gospel stories of Jesus for his model in the practice of poverty, he had to undergo an intensive learning process to determine which acts could be most effective in changing his consciousness or (what amounts to the same thing) transforming the world, rearranging the profane into the sacred. He had to learn that each moment presents its own opportunity, that nothing can be planned in advance, that moment-to-moment living is the only reliable teacher. Indeed, the God who clothes the lilies and the birds is present in each moment, giving Francis the circumstances and the challenge wherein the spiritual response of poverty is to be discovered. Every moment is potentially an opportunity for an exchange with God. God speaks in providing the circumstances, Francis responds by giving something away. A divine/human dialogue occurs in every moment of time. To be conscious of this and to act upon it is to abolish profane time and open up the sacred timelessness of God's world.

His earliest biographers like to imply that Francis's life reiterated some of the main themes and even the miracles of Jesus' life, but it would be more accurate to say that he was an original. He did not so much imitate the things Jesus did as discover for himself through relentless experimentation how the cosmos of Jesus could be established and lived in thirteenth century Italy.

The Bishop's Cloak

Francis's great reversal of values began with almost liturgical drama when he spurned his father in the presence of the bishop. A "miracle" had occurred: the wooden Christ on a crucifix had ordered him to "Repair my church." Promptly selling a quantity of cloth and a horse belonging to his father, he offered the money to the pastor of that church. The pastor refused, the father sued, and Francis went into hiding. After the money was recovered, Pietro brought his son before the bishop "to renounce all his claims and return everything he had." Francis promptly stripped off the clothes he was wearing, gave them to his father, and in his nakedness declared:

> "Until now I have called you my father, but from now on I can say without reserve, 'Our Father who art in heaven.' He is all my wealth and I place my confidence in him." When the bishop heard this, he was amazed at his passionate fervor. He jumped to his feet and took Francis into his embrace, covering him with the cloak he was wearing, like the good man that he was (*MajLife*: II, 4).[2]

There are variants of this story in the several early biographies, but the message clearly remains that Francis rejected the civil authorities under which his father had sued him in favor of churchly authority in the person of the bishop. The fatherhood of God was decisively to be mediated by the church. But the church, too, became a problematic father (or mother) for the young man who was determined to live a personal dialogue with God through choosing to be poor. There is a religio-political tension in the imagery of the scene. The bishop is awed by Francis's fervor, that radical passion that apparently cares nothing for what people may think, and that burns his bridges behind him. He has given up all material and profane security. His stripping off of his clothes might have been a perfect religious act—except for his nakedness. Standing there exposed, he is also an embarrassment. His passionate fervor has something risqué about it, and the bishop hastens to hide Francis's nakedness behind his ecclesiastical cloak.

This is only the first and by no means the last time Francis came close to embarrassing the church. He and his followers too closely resembled other mystic bands who practiced a form of poverty but had been declared heretics, the Cathars and Waldensians. The heretics made the church their enemy, opposed the priesthood, and denied the efficacy of the sacraments when they were administered by lax or sinful priests. Francis, despite his grubby appearance and rebellious attitude, however, had no intention of repudiating the church but only of reforming it. He was critical of its wealth, its compromise with the kingdom of this world, and particularly of the religious orders whose monasteries had become landholders, even to the point of commanding small armies of knights.[3] He also spurned learning and the intricacies of theological argument. But he spoke so eloquently of his love of God and "holy poverty" that crowds wept and people from all walks of life gave away their possessions so as to wander dusty mountain roads with growling stomachs and happy hearts.

In the space of the two decades that elapsed between his repudiation of his father and his death, he won tens of thousands of followers and formulated an emotional Christianity that appealed to the townspeople and the uneducated dregs of society which the official church, with its tilt toward the nobility, had overlooked. In retrospect, we can see that he changed the direction of Western Christianity while inspiring legends that are still being told today.

By the time of Francis's death at the age of forty-five, however, it looked as though the spirit of his rebellion had been entirely absorbed and corrupted by the church he had tried to serve. His most influential followers were building grand cathedrals and assuming professorships at the Universities of Oxford and Paris, while those who attempted to continue a life of absolute poverty were reviled as fanatics and suspected of heresy. The little towns of north Italy fought over his disease-ridden body like vultures, determined to secure fame and wealth by displaying his relics once he was dead. "By the next century, Franciscans were attracting donations from the wealthy, and knights and ladies were having themselves buried in Franciscan habits" (Tuchman, 1978: 31).

Very likely the reason Francis of Assisi is known today as a saint rather than a heretic is the relationship he cultivated with Pope Innocent III who gave verbal (non-written) approval for the foundation of a religious order designed to perpetuate the way of life Francis and his eleven earliest followers were living. Although the fact of this approval was never doubted, the nature of what was approved became the center of a controversy in the last years of Francis's life leading to an official promulgation of the Franciscan Rule of Life which differs substantially from the ideals of the earliest band of friars. The entire Franciscan movement had found itself covered by the bishop's cloak. In the two decades that elapsed between Francis's personal conversion to a life of absolute poverty and the establishment of his religious order, a potentially disruptive movement of enormous proportions was tamed and assimilated to social and ecclesiastical norms that were a horror to its charismatic founder.

We may therefore view with some suspicion the rapid canonization process whereby Francis was declared a saint of the Catholic church only two years after his death. The church admitted no contradiction between beatifying the man and revising his doctrines. Instead it hurried to craft an official version of his life, a tamed and watered-down account, designed to manage the lives of his far-flung disciples, the vast majority of whom had never met him. Just as the town of Assisi gained possession of his bones and built a cathedral over them, the authorities in Rome secured possession of his life-story by commissioning a talented rhetorician, Thomas of Celano, a learned friar who was never a companion of Francis to write his official biography.

Celano finally wrote three "Lives" of St. Francis, or "legends" (*legendae*), that is writings that were meant to be read aloud for the public to hear (from *legere*, Latin, "to read"). Each was more filled with miracles than the last. Within the two decades after Francis's death, when Celano was writing his biographies, three other "legends" appeared. Two of them were apparently written by Francis's close associates (*The Legend of the Three Companions* and *The Legend of Perugia*). The third (*The Holy Intercourse of Francis and His Lady Poverty*), which was written before *1Celano*, is a religious allegory by an unknown Franciscan.

A quarter of a century after the death of Francis, even the Franciscans were fighting over his identity, each faction employing its favorite biography to make its points. Therefore, in 1260, at a "General Chapter," that is a comprehensive meeting of the order to determine its goals and objectives, its Minister General, St. Bonaventure, an influential theologian of mysticism, was asked to write an "official biography," what has become known as his *Major Life of St. Francis* (*Legenda maior*), completed in 1263. Borrowing from all the biographies then known, he compiled a saint's life in which Francis's formulaic greeting was, "May the Lord give you his peace" (*MajLife*: III, 2); and he ordered his followers to, "Go and proclaim peace to men and preach repentance for the forgiveness of sins" (*MajLife*: III, 7). If Francis was primarily a man of peace, his Franciscans could hardly claim to be following him if they continued to foment discord. And to ensure that this be the case—the final cloak—Franciscans were ordered to burn all earlier biographies, which they apparently did. We have copies of them today only because some non-Franciscan monasteries had no obligation to destroy them.

With the hindsight of the twenty-first century, we can see that the stories of Francis must have been growing and becoming progressively more fantastic like folklore. The image of Francis people remembered was bound to become less and less distinct, as more and more was claimed about him. Bonaventure's effort preserved a nucleus of anecdotes deemed officially acceptable and gave a definite form to the Francis of faith—though it is hardly what we would call a dependable biography in any modern sense. No less than Celano or Francis's closest companions, Bonaventure has larded every anecdote with biblical phrases designed to impress us with the orthodoxy and divine guidance that transformed the impractical, fun-loving, and dreamy adolescent Francesco di Bernardone into St. Francis of Assisi. Ultimately there is no getting behind the legends to the "real, historical Francis." The only Francis we have is the charismatic and legendary figure that inspired the anecdotes, the Francis who lives on in the hearts and minds of those who have been gripped by his story.

Brother Jacoba

Despite all efforts in the direction of orthodoxy, a number of curious anecdotes have survived. One of the most intriguing of these concerns a noble widow from Rome, Lady Jacoba di Settesoli. No mention is made of her before Francis is on his deathbed, when he requests a letter be written. He wants to see her one last time, and he wants her to bring gray shroud cloth and some of the honey-almond confection he loves. No sooner is the letter written, than there is a knock at the gate, and Jacoba is there with the cloth and the sweet. Immediately there is a problem: should this woman be allowed inside the cloister to see the dying saint? Francis brushes the issue aside. This woman is an exception to the rule. He calls her "Brother Jacoba" (*Perugia*: 101; *Mirror*: 112).

The story may have been preserved as "evidence" of a minor miracle, the fact that Jacoba appears with the desired objects as soon as Francis has his wishes written down. But it is not at all clear from the context how this "miracle" has anything to do with sainthood. We fail even to learn what possessed the pious lady to make the several-day trip precisely at that time. Had she been given a dream or vision, or merely an inspired hunch? From our present-day perspective we can appreciate the extraordinary nature of Lady Jacoba's arrival without having to think it was miraculous. It is similar to our infrequent but familiar experience of finding ourselves thinking about someone just as that very person rings us up. Such events are most likely to happen when there is a powerful emotional connection between the two individuals. They are likely to be lovers, parent and child, or something of the kind. The mystical literature is full of such events between guru and disciple[4]; and the biographers of Edgar Cayce report many instances when the "sleeping prophet" would perform one of his entranced cure-readings on a individual who—unbeknownst to Cayce—had just mailed a request for such a seance.[5]

The evidence seems unmistakable that Jacoba's relationship with Francis is long-standing and deep, undoubtedly bearing an erotic cast which both *Perugia* and *Mirror* seem to confirm in describing her as a "Mary Magdalen," "in that she had received the gift of tears and fervor from God." Francis wants to see her one last time and to be buried in her shroud. Furthermore, her status as "Brother Jacoba" implies that she has long enjoyed an exception to the general rule of cloister. Another tradition goes so far as to say Francis was able to recognize only two women by their faces—Clare and Jacoba—for he was in the habit of lowering his eyes when obliged to speak to women (Erickson, 1970: 84f).

Thomas of Celano, in his third "Life," gives an extended account of this final meeting between Francis and Jacoba (*3Celano*: 37–39). She was about to send her retinue away so as to stay with Francis until the end, but he tells her he will die on Saturday and that she can continue her journey on Sunday. It happens as he predicted, and she is with him at the end.

> She was led quietly, streaming with tears, to Francis, and his body was placed in her arms. "See," said the vicar, "he whom you loved in life you shall hold in your arms in death." She wept hot tears over his body, wept aloud, and sighed deeply; and holding him in her arms and kissing him, she loosened the veil so that she would see him unhindered. Why should we say more? She looked upon that precious body in which also a precious treasure lay hidden, ornamented as it was with five pearls (*Ibid.*, 39).

Suddenly Jacoba is no longer Mary Magdalen, the sinner who loved much. She has become the sinless one, Mary the Mother of Jesus. We are looking at a pieta. The "five pearls" ornamenting the naked body in her arms are Francis's stigmata, the wounds in his hands, feet, and side.

Francis's life of reversal begins and ends in nakedness. At the beginning, when he strips in front of the bishop, he chooses God as his only father. At the end, when his "veil" is loosened by Jacoba and falls away, we see that God has fully and dramatically accepted Francis. He bears the crucifixion marks of the Son of God. In its monotheism, Christianity could never say that Francis was an *avatar*, another incarnation of the godhead; but the imagery employed by his hagiographers implies a theologically chaste divinization.

As far as we know, Francis was the first stigmatic. The psychosomatic appearance of the wounds of crucifixion is more understandable to us today, when celebrated individuals like Padre Pio and hundreds of lesser known Christians have been studied. We know that a powerful cultural image can operate in the unconscious to effect changes in the body. Although the manifestation of stigmata remains extremely rare, its occurrence is well-known and functions as a cultural suggestion which may be seized upon by any person who is adequately predisposed. Again, however, Francis was an original. In 1224 there was no precedent for such an event. It seemed to his contemporaries, and probably to Francis himself, that he had been singled out by God for a unique physical ratification of his saintly life. Everyone who knew him was aware that he had striven over two full decades to live a life of perfect poverty in imitation of Jesus. Now it was evident by divine miracle that he had succeeded in the eyes of God. He was unquestionably a second Christ.

Loosening the Veil

For us inhabitants of the twenty-first century to loosen the veil around Francis means to drop our cultural assumptions and to attempt to reconstruct for ourselves the psychology of his mystical practice. While his biographers sought to reveal his sanctity by assembling biblical texts and theological propositions, we will attend to the events depicted in the stories themselves and ask what are the psychological dynamics occurring in Francis himself when he was doing these things. We want to know what techniques he was using to transform the profane world into the sacred. How must things have looked and felt to Francis when he danced and sang and preached to the birds?

When I speak of our cultural assumptions that must be loosened and allowed to drop, I mean not only the Christian form that Western culture has had over the past two millennia, but also the Cartesian and Newtonian perspectives that cut us off from the mind of the Middle

Ages. To some extent, it would be easier for us to understand Francis if he had been a Hindu, for then the exotic nature of his origins would allow us more easily to lay aside our modern Western mind-set.

Indeed, if he had been a Hindu, we would probably conclude that he was an avatar of Shiva, the Lord of Reversal, the god who destroys the universe to reveal a larger Reality, the Lord of Yoga, the unrespectable god who loves to be intoxicated and overturns all conventions, who goes about naked and smeared with the ashes of cremation grounds, the Lord of the Dance, the Lord of the Animals, the God of Sex who makes love to Parvati, the Lady of the Mountain, for thousands of years on end without ejaculating. For Francis used poverty to effect a grand reversal that destroyed the profane world and revealed a sacred cosmos; he loved nothing more than meditating; he was reviled as a heretic, a reprobate, and ne'er-do-well; he was naked at the beginning and the end of his story as well as several times in the middle; otherwise, he wore the most patched and flea-infested clothes he could find; he called Death his sister; he communicated with birds, mammals, fish, and insects; he sang and danced in his intoxication with God; and all of his biographers aver that he was betrothed, married, or constantly making love to Lady Poverty,[6] the Lady of the Mountain, although this was a chaste form of love-making. Francis is said to have slept sitting up and meditating, reminding us of a yogi spending the night in *samadhi* (at one with the Absolute), drifting in and out of sleep without losing God-consciousness (*1 Celano*: 52). But perhaps the most unexpected tradition holds that Brother Juniper responded to Brother Tendelbene's death by saying that he would like to turn the dead friar's skull into a bowl and cup for his daily use (Englebert, 1979: 99). The followers of Shiva are famous for using skulls for precisely this purpose.

If we can remember parallels such as these, we will certainly have loosened the veil of Christian piety that conceals the mystical psychology of Francis of Assisi. Because Francis's experience and behavior so much resemble those of another culture's divine model, there must be something universally human about his style of mysticism. Both the Hindu and Francis employ the same instrument in their sadhana (or "spiritual practice"), namely the thing that is closest to hand, their body-and-mind. It is true that Francis referred to his body as Brother Ass, and he meant that it was the source of his temptations to return to the profane world of everyday comforts. But he read his body's reactions and kept a close watch on his emotional and physiological responses to the situations, people, and events with which life presented him. Indeed, this is another meaning in Brother Jacoba's unveiling. She shows us the instrument, beatified by its extraordinary marks, by which he achieved his ecstasies—those emotional and physiological states that made it possible for him to live in the sacred cosmos.

THREE

The Spiritual Practice of Poverty

Francis . . . was a merchant
who bought the pearl of the Gospel Life,
selling and giving away all he had
for the sake of Christ. (*MajLife*: XI, 14)

S AINTS' LIVES (HAGIOGRAPHY) constitute a genre all their own. The writer is concerned to emphasize the sanctity and exemplary nature of a religious hero. Purely human details that would be quite important in a modern biography are avoided in favor of seemingly extraordinary details, told in such a way as to imply supernatural agency, miraculous interventions, and signs of divine favor. Generally the work begins with an account of the sinfulness and spiritual ignorance of the future saint's early days. This is followed by a painful and dramatic conversion experience which sets the stage for decades of self-abnegation and unremitting holiness in which miraculous events become more and more frequent until martyrdom or a beatific passing crowns a life designed to inspire us all. After death there is usually a spate of miracles and pious recollections that strain the credulity of modern readers, all in justification of papal canonization, the infallible declaration that the subject now unquestionably lives in heaven with God and therefore can be a reliable model for the rest of us.

Although the "Lives" of Francis follow this plan quite closely, it is noteworthy that nothing particularly sinful has been remembered from his early life. He was a high-spirited, fun-loving scamp both before and after his conversion—talented at organizing parties, games, and songs. By some accounts his pre-conversion eccentricity reached nearly to the point of clownery, while prefiguring his post-conversion behavior: "Sometimes . . . [he] would insist on the richest cloth and the commonest [be] sewn together in the same garment" (*L3Comps*: 2). His playful grandiosity sought to compensate his commoner's birth by flamboyantly spending his father's money in acts of generosity. Compared to the nobles he knew, he was "poorer in matter of wealth, but more lavish in giving things away" (*1Celano*: 4). In short, he was a spendthrift and squanderer both before and after his conversion.

The difference lies not in his prodigality but in his motives. Formerly he sought approval of his friends and dreamed of distinguishing himself as a knight—not so much as a warrior but as a splendid figure. His father must have looked on with ambivalence, proud of his son's courtly ways yet worried about his heedlessness. Even selling his father's possessions so as to "repair my church" belongs to his life before sainthood insofar as it cost him nothing. Indeed, had the gambit succeeded it would not have been Francis who had repaired the church but his father. He was seeking to fulfill the command in a merely formal and literal manner, taking no personal responsibility, running and hiding from his father. Instead of taking a stand he was bobbing and weaving. Only when his father cornered him before the bishop did he finally take the step that opened up his saintly future.

In this way the biographers make it clear that the "sinful" son of Pietro underwent a psychological reversal of some sort and redirected his attention from an outer world to an inner, from social approval to a sense of inner coherence. They are rather vague, though, about how he got to this point. The wooden statue of Christ spoke to him only after he had already been seeking out-of-the-way places in which to pray. What brought that on? We are given only one inadequate incident by way of explanation. One day when Francis was tending his father's store, he refused a beggar who requested "alms for the love of God." Shortly thereafter he bitterly regretted his action, realizing that he would have given the man something, had he asked "in the name of some great prince" (*L3Comps*: 3). Already guilt formulates the theme of his saintly life: an earthly prince versus "the King of kings and Lord of All." We are not told how he got to the point of seeing life as a contest between a pair of competing kingdoms. Certainly it was a common medieval metaphor. But how many, after all, took it seriously? To found one's life-decisions on the premise that the kingdom of heaven is real and viable here and now, if only we can banish the world of common sense, already suggests a candidate for sainthood. The hagiographers, therefore, give us an unconscious saint before the conversion and a conscious saint afterward. None of them had known the old Francis. Whatever fragments of rumor they had heard about his earlier life were naturally interpreted within the context of the religious hero they came to know years later.

Before the change of heart, he was struggling to craft a joyous life free of worldly cares. Eventually some incident, such as the one with the beggar, alerted him to the fact that God had to be an important factor in the struggle, and he began to seek deserted places in which to pray. Apparently he did not at first discontinue his partying, spendthrift ways or his compulsion to make himself look good in the eyes of others. Indeed, his stripping before the bishop might have been an impetuous act, made on the spur of the moment, possibly out of anger because his "honor" had been challenged. He may have tricked himself into taking on poverty as a way of life and had not the faintest idea that it could become a sadhana, a spiritual practice. Too proud and obstinate to relinquish the plan of repairing the rundown chapel—or possibly intimidated by a God who could make a wooden statue speak—he began begging the stones and other materials he needed to rebuild it with his own hands. His life of genuine poverty had begun, though he did not yet grasp what it meant.

Reversal of Values

Although discovering the nature of spiritual poverty and what it could do for his body-and-mind surely involved a process of experimentation that lasted several years, it is certain that the notion of having no possessions recommended itself to Francis in the beginning on account of the gospel stories of Jesus. Poverty was the most obvious characteristic of the day-to-day life of Jesus, who had been born in a manger and throughout his public life had had "no place to lay his head." Poverty, Francis said, "has Christ" (*2Celano*: 84). Therefore, he instructed his followers to glimpse the sacred in every hungry and ill-clothed person they met. "When you see a poor man, Brother, an image is placed before you of the Lord and his poor mother" (*2Celano*: 85). The poorer the man, apparently, the more of Christ, for Francis found himself envious of travelers more ragged than he was. He eagerly exchanged garments with them, or clothed them in his own robe, going naked until chance should supply a replacement (*Mirror*: 34).

At least in the beginning, poverty functioned as a sort of badge for Francis. On the one hand, it amounted to a public declaration, a silent act of preaching by which he hoped to model for others a life founded in God-consciousness. On the other hand, putting on the most despised of tunics and robes constituted a personal act of mindfulness. He engaged in a daily ritual of vesting himself in the garments of a cosmos wholly at odds with the world of public opinion. Just as a preliterate tribesman dons the paraphernalia of the gods or culture heroes celebrated in his tribe's mythology and then dances his way into an ecstatic identification with those sacred personages, so Francis put on the ragged garments of those who, like the lilies and the birds, had nothing to depend upon but God.

He must have discovered very early in his sadhana of poverty that trading downward was a most effective technique of ecstasy. *The Legend of the Three Companions* formulates this very convincingly as God's answer to Francis's prayer:

> [God says:] "O Francis, if you want to know my will, you must hate and despise all that which hitherto your body has loved and desired to possess. Once you begin to do this, all that formerly seemed sweet and pleasant to you will become bitter and unbearable; and instead, the things that formerly made you shudder will bring you great sweetness and content (*L3Comps*: 11).

Perhaps Francis actually heard these words with his inner ear. If not, they are at least central to what his closest "three companions" remembered about him. For whatever *God* says is bound to be important; and if God has something to say about awareness of our body-and-mind, we will have to take these pointers very seriously, indeed. In this passage we are given the internal criteria for Francis's life of reversal. What "formerly seemed sweet and pleasant" and "your body desired" will become repugnant; and the horrifying will become sweet and fulfilling.

As far as our feelings are concerned, the sacred world is just the opposite of this one. The things we look forward to here are what hold us here; and we will know when the reversal has occurred, for then those same things will have become repugnant. We will have no taste for them, for it is they that pull us back from the ecstatic world. Similarly, what we find "bitter and unbearable," the things that make us "shudder" here in the conventional world are but hidden gateways to the kingdom of God, and therefore promise to bring us "great sweetness and content." The words ascribed to God in this incident redirect our attention to how things feel and illustrate how it is that the body-and-mind we always have with us is the key to transforming the world. Unfortunately, however, for most of us nothing is more habitual than overlooking and downplaying the reactions of our body-and-mind. In contrast, Francis constructed a disciplined religious practice upon the reactions of his body-and-mind. By attending to what we habitually discard, he learned to convert the events of every-day life into the means of transcending them.

Having started out with the idea of imitating an external model, the poverty of Jesus, a major change takes place when Francis begins looking within for guidance. We do not know how many months may have elapsed between the scene before the bishop and his discovery of the reversal of values, but there cannot have been many. Stories are told about the days when Francis was only a noteworthy eccentric, and not yet a living saint. Brothers Leo, Angelo, and Rufino, the "three companions," recall how they were "exalting and joyful in the face of the jeering and mudslinging" they received (*L3Comps*: 40). A fourth companion, Brother Bernard, who had formerly been a wealthy nobleman, explains, "It is true we are poor, but to us poverty is not the burden it is to others for we have become poor voluntarily by the grace of God" (*L3Comps*: 39).

The Joy of Poverty

The fact that the sadhana of poverty reverses all values was the first and most fundamental lesson a friar had to learn. Therefore, when Giles was seen to give "his cloak to a poor man with great cheerfulness," Francis immediately received him into the Order (*Mirror*: 36). He had passed the essential test. Because he knew the joy of poverty, he was already capable of dissolving the material world into the sacred cosmos. He already had the soul of Francis within him. This principle is most famously described in a monologue in which Francis instructs his closest companion and scribe, Brother Leo. Perfect joy, says Francis, has nothing to do with saintly accomplishments, including miracles and the conversion of infidels. Rather we know we have experienced perfect joy when we come home soaked, frozen, and weak with hunger, only to have the porter refuse us entrance, then insult us and beat us with a club.

> . . . if we endure all those evils and insults and blows with joy and patience, reflecting that we must accept and bear the sufferings of the Blessed Christ patiently for love of Him, oh, Brother Leo, write: that is perfect joy!
>
> And now hear the conclusion, Brother Leo. Above all the graces and gifts of the Holy Spirit which Christ gives to His friends is that of conquering oneself and willingly enduring sufferings, insults, humiliations, and hardships for the love of Christ. For we cannot glory in all those other marvelous gifts of God, as they are not ours but God's . . .
>
> But we can glory in the cross of tribulations and afflictions, because that is ours . . . (*Flowers*: 8).

We misunderstand a passage like this if we think Francis is saying we should "put up with" suffering and indignity. He also does not mean we should cultivate some sort of immunity to pain. He means that *when such discomfort does not disturb our joy*, then we will know that our joy is "perfect." Perfect joy is the gold standard. We know we have gained access to the sacred cosmos when our joy is imperturbable.

Clearly perfect joy is no ordinary emotion, for the joy we have in completing a project, besting an opponent, or making love to our spouse always dissolves in the face of frustration, indignity, and pain. Perfect joy is immune to the ups and downs of the conventional world because it lives elsewhere. It is the distinguishing mark of our entrance into the sacred cosmos. When handing over our cloak or automobile brings us perfect joy, we have dissolved the everyday world into a larger reality. If we pay attention to what is stirred up within us while these events are taking place, we begin to appreciate that yielding in poverty changes the world and keeps our body-and-mind in a blissful state. We are no longer "there" in the world of public opinion, but on another plane entirely. The spiritual practice of poverty is a genuine sadhana because it changes our consciousness, revealing a joyous reality beside which the everyday world appears cramped and depleted. Were it not a far more capacious, interesting, and fulfilling world, our joy would not be perfect.

The Discipline of Poverty

Churchly authorities were never comfortable with Francis's radical poverty. If they guessed its potential for consciousness changing, they might have been afraid it could spark an enthusiastic movement in which thousands might leave the church and set up a rival and "heretical" institution. Mostly they spoke diplomatically of the impracticality of absolute poverty and worried about the health of Franciscans. Knowing the bishops had barely a clue as to what he was doing, Francis answered them in pretty much their own pragmatic language:

> My Lord, [he said to the bishop,] if we had any possessions we should also be forced to have arms to protect them, since possessions are a cause of disputes and strife, and in many ways we should be hindered from loving God and our neighbor. Therefore in this life we wish to have no temporal possessions (*L3Comps*: 33).

In other words, "Don't distract us from the joys of the sacred cosmos by entangling us in the struggle for possessions." The official church was already overly entangled. Francis knew from experience that entanglement begins subtly and for the best and most rational of motives. As soon as a truly poor man becomes "almost poor" he has possessions to worry about, and his career in the sacred cosmos is seriously undermined. The biographers tell several stories in which Francis uncovered a special affection he had for a wooden cup he had carved, a blanket he slept under, and the like (*2Celano: 97; Perugia: 50; 1Celano: 52*). His response was immediate and final. As soon as he caught his affection for a material object compromising his participation in the sacred world, he destroyed it. "All that which hitherto your body has loved and desired to possess . . . will become bitter and unbearable." The price for extended periods in the ecstasy of perfect joy was eternal vigilance over his conscious states. Only by monitoring his feelings was he able to catch himself in the act of forgetting. Thus his answer to the bishop declared, in effect: "Since I cannot attend both to my awareness and to my possessions, the possessions will have to go."

In his poverty, therefore, Francis was depriving himself of nothing he wanted. He was avoiding distractions, and the most seductive of distractions are the ones that slip past our censors so that we find ourselves miles away from our goal, traveling in the wrong direction, and wondering how we got there. Poverty is a tool for dropping from our lives the clutter that keeps us unfocused. As soon as we have no possessions to keep an eye on, we are alone with our feelings and reactions. Attending to them reveals us to ourselves. It is not what we are carrying in our hands that is important, but how we feel about it, what it means to us. We rarely know what things mean to us, for it is generally only after we have lost them that we begin to explore our attachments. Usually it feels as though we have lost a part of ourselves. Until that sinking feeling overcomes us, we remain ignorant of how much of ourselves we had invested.

Francis was determined to invest nothing of himself in the world of space and time. Even the act of soaking beans overnight so that they would be ready for the next day's meal entangled the friars in providing for the future. He forbade the practice and asked them to beg only for what they would need today, to let tomorrow take care of itself (*Perugia*: 4). Left to its own devices, our ego is bound to start planning, reviewing the pantry shelves, sketching out tonight's dinner and tomorrow's breakfast. All of this entangles us in a world where we are providing for ourselves as though there were no "other world" to consider. Francis used poverty as a means to frustrate the ego's obsessions with security and material comfort.

Because the ego's tendency is always to rely on itself, to entangle itself in questions of material comfort, and to close off an open future with its incessant planning, Francis deliberately employed poverty to frustrate those entangling tendencies. Having no possessions with which to make plans, he had nothing to distract him from discovering the next day's portion of manna. Tomorrow always brings something, and to Francis's way of seeing things, whatever the morrow brings is a gift from God. The unplanned life, therefore, is lived under the guidance of the God who lavishly provides for the lilies of the field and the birds of the air.[7]

Having learned to distrust his ego through the sadhana of poverty, Francis devised further means to rein it in, and to keep himself in a state of mental receptivity. For example, when he confronted the question of whether he should devote his life to meditation or to preaching, he did not trust himself to discern God's will but asked Clare and Brother Silvester to pray over the question and let him know what they took God's will to be. They both determined that God wanted Francis to preach; and, although his own inclination was to pray, he immediately accepted their judgment, confident that it was God's will and not his own (*Flowers*: 16). Similarly, after resigning his office as Minister General of the Order, he addressed his replacement with these words: "I wish always to have at my side one of my companions who will represent your authority for me and whom I shall obey as if I were obeying you" (*Perugia*: 106). To answer to another's will is to by-pass one's own, to train oneself to listen and to respond. For God's will guides the sacred cosmos, and following it fills the spiritual practitioner with perfect joy.

Moving Between the Two Worlds

Francis's last attempt to introduce the spirit of his mystical practice into the Franciscan Rule was his "Testament," written to be a non-binding adjunct to the official document. He wanted his spiritual sons and daughters to know something about the course of his experience, how he learned the will of God experimentally—by taking action and then paying attention to how that action changed his consciousness. In its opening words, Francis's "Testament" describes the heart of that sad-hana, the transition from the conventional world to the sacred cosmos:

> This is how God inspired me, Brother Francis, to embark upon a life of penance. When I was in sin, the sight of lepers nauseated me beyond measure; but then God himself led me into their company, and I had pity on them. When I had once become acquainted with them, what had previously nauseated me became a source of spiritual and physical consolation for me. After that I did not wait long before leaving the world (Frugoni, 1998: 22).

What I have been calling the sadhana of poverty, Francis calls "a life of penance." Similarly, "in sin" means living in the conventional world, and "leaving the world" means entering the sacred cosmos. In these four sentences, Francis describes the crucial experience that taught him how to leave the world.

He paid attention to disturbing emotions, the fact that the sight of lepers nauseated him *beyond measure*. The extreme force of this reaction suggests that the reality of lepers was one of the points at which the everyday world threatened to fracture and fall apart for Francis. He wanted to suppress this panic, put it out of his mind for good. "But then God led me into their company." He fails to tells us precisely how he was led or what made him think God was behind it. He must have experienced an urgency moving him, more powerful and with a different style than his own familiar will-power. It was taking him in so loathsome a direction that he lost control of his nausea reflex. Something moved him so strongly that either he *could* not resist or else he found to his surprise that he *no longer wished* to do so.

When he found he had pity on the lepers, we know he was no longer thinking primarily of himself and his own safety and comfort. He saw human beings who were suffering, and suddenly the world- and self-fragmenting nature of leprosy had a human face and lost its uncanny threat. Even more: associating with lepers turned out to be "a source of spiritual and physical consolation." What had horrified him became "sweet."

We know very well that when we conquer a long-time irrational fear and find that what had occasioned such horror and revulsion is really no match for us, we become charged with power. It is as though we had stored up enough energy to defeat a dragon, but it turned out to be a mouse. All the left-over energy is immediately converted to joy and exaltation. We make a sudden emotional transition from being unrealistically timorous to being over-confident. Our new attitude is no more dependable than our old one. It just feels a lot better. Therefore, when Francis attends to the reactions of his body-and-mind and learns that opposing a repugnance in the conventional world can lead to a powerful joy, we might wonder about that consolation. Was it an illusory "inflation" of his ego, a self-deceptive experience of grandiosity? Or was it a genuine discovery that bears no comparison with the emotional ups and downs of ordinary people like ourselves?

Francis gives us only one indication: "After that I did not wait long before leaving the world." First, he waited. He must have pondered the elation he felt upon gaining the acquaintance of the lepers. Indeed, it must have surprised him a great deal and even been confusing. He probably wanted to know how trustworthy it was. Could a whole life-strategy be based on opposing one's uncanny feelings of conventional disgust? Evidently it did not take him long to determine that it could. Apparently the difference between the everyday experience of narcissistic grandiosity and Francis's "spiritual and physical consolation" is that our common neurotic experience has no discernible future while Francis's did.

In the grip of grandiosity, we are filled with the elation of an illusory power and may even think we are so clever that the rest of our life ought to flow smoothly and confidently—as though there will never be another obstacle for us. At the same time, however, we have no specific notion about *how* these wonderful things are going to happen. We envision no real future, we are just lost in an unfocused glow. Francis, on the other hand, appears to have glimpsed an alternate plan of life and an alternate world of experience. Evidently he has seen that the disturbing emotions that arise in the conventional world can function as portals through which the sacred universe can be gained. He has learned that a way of life is possible in which he stays alert for such disturbing emotions and then opposes his natural tendency to suppress them and run away. The gateway to the alternate cosmos is right there where it is least expected, in the pain, humiliation, and disgust of everyday.

The exemplary nature of Francis's life convinces us that the alternate cosmos he preferred to our world was no neurotic escape. As a world-construction it was superior to most. But his words imply that he never experienced himself as the constructor of that sacred cosmos. He does not know exactly *why* he visited those lepers. Something unconscious and foreign to his everyday ego moved him in a new direction, and his eyes were opened. When he glimpsed the sacred new world-construction, the vision confirmed hopes so wild he never knew he had had them. There was nothing to debate. He had to leave the world he shared with the rest of us. He had seen that the kingdom of heaven was a reality, *the* reality. He left our world without regret.

Experiments in Poverty

Except for the expression, "then God himself led me into their company," Francis's encounter with the lepers surely appears to be an experiment. Some unconscious impulse led him heroically to oppose his nausea. He then observed his reactions and made the discovery of his life. In this instance, at least, Francis discovered himself to be an intelligent pawn in God's experiment rather than himself the author of his daring move. But according to his biographers, it was not always so.

Indeed, it seems likely that the experiment with the lepers had been in Francis's mind for some time. The three companions of his earliest days tell us, for instance, that before "leaving the world" but during the time when he was seeking rundown churches and other out of the way places in which to pray he went through a period of exuberant fantasizing and painful inhibition. He imagined experiments in sainthood that he thought he would love to perform—if only he could step out of his familiar surroundings to a place where no one knew him.

> He was still living in the world though already greatly changed by divine grace; and sometimes the longing seized him for a place where, as an unknown stranger, he could give his own clothes to some beggar, taking the beggar's miserable

rags in exchange and setting out himself to beg for the love of God (*L3Comps*: 10).

Thomas of Celano says that Francis actually tried this experiment while on a pilgrimage to Rome: "Many times he would have done the same thing had he not been held back by shame before those who knew him" (*2Celano*: 8).

Probably Francis spent some weeks or months after the numinous leper incident day-dreaming of saintly exploits. Formerly he had day-dreamed of knightly deeds of derring-do, but now the emotional values have been reversed. When he was "in sin," romantic fantasies of knights made him feel good about himself. But these new day-dreams were different. He had learned that the most disturbing emotions—shame and disgust—could be portals to the sacred cosmos. So he set out bravely in his day-dreams to begin his experiments in poverty. As a beggar, he thought, he would finally be able to hold the sacred cosmos steady. He was on the verge, again, of that "certain exquisite joy" (*1Celano*: 10). But each time he found himself brought up short by shame. The tiny hole between the worlds consists of the emotion most consistently linked with the fragmentation of the self.

Each experiment to establish the sacred cosmos through acts of radical poverty came up against his shame. The doorway to the other world had posted a guard that was too powerful and too wily to be defeated once and for all. For even after Francis had taken the plunge and "left the world" in the sense that he had begun to beg for his food as well as for the stones he needed to rebuild the rundown church of San Damiano, he still had to confront his shame on a daily basis. Thus, while begging oil for the lamps of that church he had to pass through a large group of men to gain access to the house where he hoped to obtain a donation. The sight of the men filled him with "bashfulness," and he almost gave up his intention. Then he had to wrestle with the issue of his cowardice, turn himself around and go back, where he:

freely explained the cause of his bashfulness; and, in a kind of spiritual intoxication, he begged in French for oil and got it. Most fervently he stirred up everyone for the work of that church and speaking in a loud voice in French, he prophesied before all that there would be a monastery there of holy virgins of Christ (*2Celano*: 13).

The "prophecy" refers to the fact that several years later San Damiano became the home of St. Clare and her "Poor Ladies." Francis's speaking in French is a much more problematic issue. Some say his mother was French and he learned an elegant French from her, though there is no evidence to support this claim. Others suggest that he learned a serviceable French from his father who often traveled to France on business. But it is hard to doubt the word of Francis's three early companions, who say that French was "a language he delighted to speak, though he did not know it very well" (*L3Comps*: 10). Because no biographer reports that Francis's Italian countrymen failed to understand him on account of his outbursts of French, it seems probable that he spoke a Franco-Italian composite language, such as the traveling drama troops, jugglers, and troubadours used so that they could be understood pretty well in every town, without having to learn all the local dialects—a language "spoken nowhere and yet understood by all" (Englebert, 1979: 13).

Whatever the quality of the French, however, Celano clearly implies that Francis spoke the language when he was intoxicated with God; and this implicit claim is weakly supported by other biographers, who describe him gaily singing in French while traveling with his companions. Probably he spoke and sang in French during those periods when he became—vividly in his own mind—a sprightly troubadour for God, overcoming his shame at his eccentricities by playing the role of the saint he hoped to become. Whether he did so willfully or as the result of a trance-like intoxication with God, it is not always easy to decide. But it seems likely that he sometimes deliberately pushed the envelope in an attempt to escape from the conventional world and enter another, larger domain. For just as the Holy Roman Empire was German, but had French as its court language, so Francis sought to speak the lingo of a higher plane. A rise in the earthly hierarchy from the rude local dialect to the universal court language apparently symbolized for Francis the noble virtues of loyalty and courage that every knight was expected to display. Changing his language, therefore, may have been another technique of ecstasy for changing the world.[8]

In the oil-begging episode, French-speaking is a symptom of divine intoxication, the effectiveness of which is indicated by a return of Francis's courage and then the influence his intoxication has upon his listeners. And it is evident that he induced this world-altering ecstasy through his struggle with disturbing emotions: an initial bashfulness, the cowardice of turning back, the shame it caused, and then facing the crowd of men in a truly humiliating manner. For in "freely explaining the cause of his bashfulness," he lays everything before those men. He reserves no secrets about his eccentric motives, his deliberate beggarly status, his intimidation at the thought of their disapproval, and by implication the grandiose plan of sainthood that lies behind it all. The world-changing ecstasy occurs as powerfully as it does because his confrontation with his shadowy emotions has been so thorough. He enters an altered state of consciousness and begins to speak as though he is on stage. He speaks of the humiliation he has brought down on himself by exposing his own secrets. But he does so in an ecstasy of perfect joy.

The "Narcissistic" Emotions

Humiliation, grandiosity, shame, disgust: these and other powerfully disturbing states of mind belong to what I am calling the "narcissistic emotions." Here is the point at which Francis and the tantrikas of the East accomplished the Great Reversal that dissolved the profane world and brought the sacred cosmos to presence. They deliberately courted within their own psyches a *narcissistic crisis* which they then trained themselves to tolerate with equanimity and even-mindedness. *They courted a narcissistic crisis, and did so even-mindedly.*

Narcissism and *narcissistic* entered the psychoanalytic lexicon in 1911, when Freud discussed the auto-eroticism of the paranoid federal judge, Daniel Paul Schreber, and declared that prior to the Oedipal stage of development, there must be a stage of narcissism, where the subject takes himself, his own ego, his own body, as his love-object (*SE*, VII: 145). In choosing the term, *narcissism*, Freud was evoking for his readers the myth of Narcissus, the young man who fell in love with his own likeness, seen in the mirror of a pond. Three years later, in "On Narcissism," Freud argued that this redirection of libido to the ego-itself is essential to produce an ego that is strong enough and enduring enough for everyday life (*SE*, XIV: 75–6). From 1914 onward, psychoanalysts have referred to the first two years of life as the period of infantile narcissism, when a permanent ego is in development. The Narcissus of myth, it is true, drowned in his narcissism, as he tried to reach the beautiful youth he saw looking back from beneath the waters. Psychoanalysis recognized a positive value in the fascination with self, when it described the narcissistic stage of life as the time when a serviceable ego is built.

Approximately twenty years after these beginnings, Melanie Klein, the founder of what we now know as Object Relations Psychology, articulated the developmental problem of the narcissistic period of infantile life in a manner that made it recognizable when it reappears in the life of an adult. She called it the *paranoid/schizoid position*, and said it was characterized by a chaos of emotional forces related to the infant's need for nurture and stability on the one hand and fears of destruction and aggression on the other. In this "paranoid/schizoid" narcissistic period, the infant "splits" the object and at the same time "splits" its own reactions. Thus the infant responds one way to the so-called "good breast" and in an opposite fashion to the "bad breast." By seeing good and bad breast, good and bad mother—indeed everything important in life as split into good object and bad object—the infant wishes to escape from the destructive and bad version and stabilize and possess the good. As long as the infant remains in this paranoid/schizoid position, she never develops a stable and dependable ego. To do that, she must learn that the good mother and the bad mother are the same person—a depressing realization, in the sense that this means that the idealized good mother will never be had. Klein calls this realistic perception that mother is one, both good and bad, the *depressive position*. Unless the infant can hold the two sides together in the depressive position, no ego develops. And when we find adults "splitting" their lovers, analysts, parents, and children into good and bad objects, they, too, have fallen into the paranoid/schizoid position (Klein, 1932: 232–3).

Nearly half a century further on, Heinz Kohut approached the same issue in a somewhat different manner, noting that the infant is exposed to "narcissistic energies" from within, which on the one hand threaten to fragment him intolerably into viciously uncooperative pieces and on the other to fill him with heroic and even god-like qualities. In this way, Kohut redefined Klein's "split"; for him and the Self Psychology school he founded, the crucial factor is not so much the so-called object that is split, but the subject's own internal experience. On the one side stands fragmentation, annihilation, and shame; on the other, grandiosity, idealization, and inflation.

Kohut defines the task of the narcissistic period of infancy as "structuring a self," where "self" is understood to be the foundation of a reliable and coherent ego. Unintegrated narcissistic energies threaten the ego's coherence with feelings of fragmentation and chaos, the panicky sense that I have lost myself, that I am permanently and fatally flawed, that I may never be myself again. Or else the individual takes off in unrealistic flights of grandiosity and self-importance (Kohut, 1971).

This, then, is what I mean by "narcissistic crisis." Francis and the tantrikas of the East sought out and courted this disorder and fragmentation, placing themselves at the brink of breakdown or self-annihilation, where the flaw in the "self-synthesis" (Kohut) is in danger of tearing apart once and for all. Every one of these spiritual geniuses heroically placed herself deliberately at the brink of madness and destruction until some force that seemed wholly other to the ego—call it Kundalini, if you like—emerged and autonomously reversed the process. Francis and the tantrikas sought out experiences that threatened them with an existential crisis through the arousal of seemingly uncontrollable emotions, those of terror, disgust, lust, shame, grandiosity—what I call the narcissistic emotions. And they did so in the counter-intuitive expectation that an autonomous process—perhaps initiated by God, perhaps activated by forces that had been slumbering within the self—would effect a Great Reversal, whereby the good object and the bad would become one, the profane world would be dissolved, the narcissistic energies be channeled, and a scene of transcendent coherence and meaning would supervene. This sporting at the brink of self-annihilation is what I call "courting a narcissistic crisis."

Now we can consider the attitude that withstands the crisis: "even-mindedness." Equanimity has many antecedents, perhaps beginning with Aristotle's *apatheia*, as equilibrium and freedom from disturbance. Francis and the tantrikas place themselves before the most disturbing emotions in the human repertoire and then resist their influence. In the tradition of depth psychology, probably the first to allude to this principle was the Parisian hypnotist and alienist, Pierre Janet, who made it the foundation of his mature psychology that psychic energy (*force mentale*) is characterized by both quantity and tension. Every tendency to take action comes with a certain punch, a certain "quantity" of energy. But holding the "tension" of that punch and utilizing it for higher purposes is the engine of psychological growth. Instead of battering down the wall that opposes me by the sheer quantity of my energy, I might calmly use some of that energy to reconnoiter and determine that there is a much easier way to my goal, a window or a door not far away, perhaps the materials for fashioning a ladder (Janet, 1903).

"Holding the tension" became the watchword of C. G. Jung, who counted Pierre Janet and "the French School" the first source of inspiration behind his own school of Analytical Psychology (Haule, 1984). Jung held that "integration" and psychological growth occur when life presents one with a challenging obstacle that splits one's consciousness so that one does not know whether to go forward or back, right or left. Both alternatives have their advantages, and both their drawbacks. There being no rational solution to the problem, Jung found that if one can hold the tension between the opposites, an irrational solution will finally appear, directed from the unconscious by the mysterious agency he termed the "transcendent function." Holding still while not denying either alternative appears to stimulate the unconscious psyche to come up with a solution that emerges from out of nowhere, from the "unconscious" (Jung, 1928/48).

This describes what I mean when I say the tantrikas cultivated even-mindedness. They courted the strongest emotions in the human toolkit, emotions that tend to split our very being, right down to its roots in the earliest efforts at self-synthesis that occurred during the narcissistic period of our infancy, in the first two years of our lives. Francis and the tantrikas deliberately split themselves, and even-mindedly held onto both halves of the split until the "transcendent function" within them initiated the Great Reversal, and the profane gave way to the sacred.

Pierre Janet named the energic result of this transcendent reversal. He called it *gaspillage*, "squandering" (Janet, 1926). The narcissistic crisis stirs up vast quantities of psychic energy, sends the autonomic nervous system into overdrive; and then, when Francis simply holds still and refuses to act, his excess energy cascades into gratifying emotions of fulfillment and transcendent meaning. Although Janet was doubtful that much good could come of mystical states, I think he got the dynamics right. In his even-mindedness, Francis does not squander the energy he has aroused in anxious dithering. He lets it pour over into his unconscious, where it transforms his world.

Further Uses of Shame
Francis's focus on his conscious states did not end at the point that he faced down his shame and squeezed through into the sacred cosmos. A number of stories indicate that he continued to attend to his feelings even after slipping through the gap between the worlds. He is said, for example, to have detected "vainglory" after giving his mantle to an old woman (*2Celano*: 132; *Perugia*: 41). The self-congratulation of vainglory recreates the world of public opinion and makes the sacred world vanish. Pride reconstitutes the everyday ego. Narcissistic emotions banish the sacred cosmos when their tension cannot be held.[9] There is nothing for Francis to do but to confront his vainglory; and he does so immediately and in a manner that courts powerful feelings of shame. He confesses his unworthy and anti-saintly state of inflation to everyone who will listen. Again he publicly abases himself upon seeing that he has missed an opportunity to reverse his consciousness and "leave the world." It might be considered a masochistic move, in that Francis derives pleasure from the act of publicly humiliating himself. But if so, we would expect to find a shrillness in the emotion of shame, that give-away trait of a neurotic reaction. We would expect no insight into the nature of shame, no sorting out of types of shame. Francis, however, made himself an expert in shame.

He taught his followers the technique of attending to their shame, saying that "shame is the enemy of salvation" and that they should not be "confused by shame" (*2Celano*: 71). Shame confuses because it obliterates the sacred plane while re-establishing the conventional world. On the other hand, one might legitimately be ashamed to "preach penance," i.e., the sadhana of poverty, knowing that one is "ignorant and of no account." Although this is a realistic shame, in that no one is worthy of preaching penance, one must not give in to it but rather use it to remind oneself that, in preaching, one is merely God's instrument. One must be willing to "suffer [insult and injury] humbly and patiently" while trusting in God—that greater agency that takes over when one's egohood has been set aside (*L3Comps*: 36). When his companions came back from begging and were happily joking and vying with one another over who had gathered the richest supply, "Blessed Francis rejoiced to see them gay and happy" (*Perugia*: 3). He saw that they had broken through the shame barrier and inhabited the realm of that "certain exquisite joy" that betokens the sacred cosmos. In his spiritual guidance, he monitored their feelings in the same manner that he attended to his own.

Shame can also function as a hindrance to spiritual progress and was therefore not always to be confronted directly. For example, new recruits to the Order were not sent out to beg immediately, for "they would blush" (*Perugia*: 3). Thus in the beginning Francis did all the begging himself and later on monitored the progress of novices to see when they were firm enough in their psychological and spiritual development to be able to take on the shame of begging. He also perceived that the community of friars constituted its own form of the consensual world, where expectations regarding the rigors of poverty and fasting were much more stringent than those of the larger public. This placed his friars under extraordinary pressure to deny their everyday needs. Therefore, when he found a brother who was "dying of hunger" due to his zeal in fasting, Francis roused the entire community in the middle of the night and got everyone eating so that the undernourished brother would be able to eat what he needed and "would not blush" (*Perugia*: 1). On another occasion, he took an old, sick brother to a vineyard and began eating grapes himself "so that the brother would not be ashamed to eat them alone" (*Perugia*: 5). He forbade a scrupulous brother to confess his sins, "because his shame at confessing them every day aggravated his torment" (*Perugia*: 7)

Finally, shame may occur when one is already inhabiting the sacred domain, where the narcissistic emotion may operate as a warning against complacency.

I am greatly ashamed when I meet someone poorer than myself. I chose holy poverty and made her my Lady, my delight, my spiritual and temporal treasure. God and all mankind know that I profess poverty. I ought to blush for shame when I meet someone poorer than myself (*Perugia*: 88).

We might rephrase this confession as follows. The sadhana of poverty is like wooing a beautiful woman. When you bring her flowers every day and do what you believe to be your utmost to make her happy, you may feel good about your relationship. But the day you discover than someone else has planted a flower garden in her backyard and tends it beautifully, you realize there is more that you could have been doing. You have unconsciously set a limit to your devotion, and this has allowed another suitor to put you to shame. Francis speaks similarly when he says to his followers, "I wish to be filled with shame before you if at any time I do nothing of these three things": thinking, speaking, and doing what is holy (*2Celano*: 159).

Narcissism and Sainthood

Freud coined the term "narcissism" in reference to the Greek myth of Narcissus and the tall flower usually found bending over its reflection in a pool or stream. Freud meant to imply a love of oneself, the image of Narcissus, who drowned trying to reach the watery young man of his reflection. He had fallen in love with himself while believing his beloved to be a stranger.

When Francis caught himself indulging in vainglory after giving his mantle to the old woman, he was horrified to discover that he was loving himself. The ideal of giving things away "for the love of God" had served only as a self-deceptive cover to hide the fact that he was redirecting the glory to himself. Libido from the unconscious, ostensibly aroused by a desire to practice the sadhana of poverty for the love of God, had "cathected" his ego—had attached itself to his ego, as to a beloved. What inwardly felt like love for another was in fact nothing more than love of himself.

Libido from our unconscious *must* attach itself to the ego if we are to have sufficient self-respect to lead a normal life. But when we cannot escape a preoccupation with ourselves, narcissism has become a problem. Francis seems to have grasped this principle when he selected shame as the primary emotion to monitor in his spiritual practice.

For shame is the emotion that betrays substantial loss of self-esteem. Francis kept his novices back from a direct challenge to the shame that would surely have been provoked by their going out to beg before they had developed a healthy level of self-esteem in their new identity as friars. He knew some "ego-building" was required.

Shame inspires us all to do our best to win the applause of society. It makes us feel worthless and drives us to do all we can to garner social approval in hopes that the praise of others will compensate for the self-regard we cannot muster within ourselves. As such it is the enemy of anyone who wants to make a transit between worlds. Shame and its narcissistic solution, striving for the praise of others, anchors the world of public opinion and blocks our way elsewhere. When Francis was "still in sin," he appears to have been primarily interested in winning the regard of his partying comrades, the bourgeois twenty-somethings of Assisi in the first decade of the thirteenth century. Because he had a reputation for knowing how to throw a party, his neurotic solution was probably successful. He was probably too happily popular to have any reason to notice the central dishonesty in his life. He was striving for applause because something was gravely amiss. Whatever came before his world-changing encounter with the lepers, it must have involved an honest look at the dread lurking below his gaiety and pretense. At bottom, Francis became a saint because he dared to acknowledge his narcissism, honestly assess what he saw, and institute a life-long series of experiments to challenge its hold on his consciousness.

Narcissistic issues have to do with the stability of the personality as a whole, the "self," a much larger reality than the ego. The fragility of narcissism, the tendency to fear I am worthless, empty at the core, and split into fragments by powerful emotions may then be described as symptoms of a self that lacks coherent structure.[10] Beneath every well-functioning ego, there must be a coherently structured self providing a floor of stability.

Because none of us is immune to moments—or even lengthy episodes—in which the floor of stability seems to have been pulled out from under us, no one can boast of a fully integrated and coherent self-structure. Under the right conditions any of us can fall into the confusion of shame, become inflated with feelings of grandiosity, nauseated with disgust, carried away from ourselves by lust, or otherwise devastated by uncontrollable emotion. While our habitual integration will be sufficient for most occasions, under the right provocation any of us can fall apart. Whether well or poorly integrated, each of us has a narcissistic flaw in our self-structure.

Flirting with Dissolution

Although Francis surely lacked a language to talk about these things, it seems evident that he knew the central principle very well. He found the frenetic effort to win social acclaim to be hollow and changed tactics. He replaced the applause of his comrades with a strategy of biblical experiments, exchanging clothes with beggars in foreign locales, where the shame factor was substantially reduced. Here, he found that shame—that is to say, narcissism—was the issue. However biblically inspired the stunts he contrived, he was always stuck fast in the conventional world by his dread of what people might say. He could not escape from the neurotic strategy of narcissism, which reasserted itself under all conditions.

In the first phase of his life, when he was "in sin," he was driven by a fear of narcissistic crisis. He was running from shame. The second stage began when he tried to redirect his course through biblical experiments but discovered that shame was still the obstacle. Here, he tried to outsmart shame by choosing foreign locales for his experiments. The third stage of his life, the point he describes as "leaving the world," began with a crucial reversal of his mindset. Instead of trying to run from shame or to outsmart it, he took shame as his advisor. He found that deeply disturbing narcissistic emotions were always located at cross-over points between the worlds, just where most of us turn tail and run. It is terrifying to contemplate the dissolution of the self I have always known as well as the world it has constructed. But for a new world and a new self to come into existence, the old must disintegrate. In his confrontation with shame, Francis discovered he had to allow his "sinful" self and the "sinful" world to fall apart and disappear so that a new experimental self could assemble itself in the sacred cosmos.

Because my narcissistic wound is the place where the coherence of self and of world is fatally challenged, it is the point where I feel absolutely powerless. There is nothing I, the conscious ego, can do about the unintegrated and incoherent sector of my self. I am certainly unable to hold it together, for it is more comprehensive than I. The self is what holds *me* together, if anything does. I can try to distract myself from the crisis by stirring up applause—i.e., splitting the problem off from consciousness—but ultimately I am helpless. My best hope is to stop trying to control the situation and wait to see what happens. If my self is not too deeply flawed—and chances are it is not—I will shortly learn that it has the capacity to pull me together on its own.

> A dissociation will not be healed by being split off, but by more complete disintegration. All the powers that strive for unity, all healthy desire for selfhood, will resist the disintegration, and in this way he will become conscious of the possibility of an inner integration, which before he had always sought outside himself. He will then find his reward in an undivided self (Jung, 1926: ¶334).

The great lesson in Jung's life occurred a few years before he wrote these lines. The break-up with Freud had opened his narcissistic wound, bringing on psychotic-like symptoms that lasted several years. He had to remind himself frequently of his identity, family, and responsibilities in hopes of keeping one foot in the conventional world. Although he felt in danger of entering the psychotic world forever, he did not directly fight the process. He tried to learn from the powerful dream-like fantasies he was having. Eventually, about six years before writing the passage quoted above, he found that his psyche pulled itself back together again, with renewed direction and greater creativity. Out of this experience, he developed his theory of the self as the psyche's ultimate principle of organization (Jung, 1961: 170–99).

The remarkable thing is that Francis seems to have learned pretty much the same lesson. For his sadhana consisted in attending to states of consciousness that signaled the immanent dissolution of self-and-world. He had learned that what supported the "world of sin" was any denial of an impending narcissistic crisis. He kept himself on guard to resist his natural inclination to flee from any shameful truth about himself. His great reversal began by acknowledging the emotion that posed the existential threat. He confessed it to himself and to his associates, and kept it fully in mind while he carried out the experiment that had provoked it. He found that entering right into his shame brought about "a more complete disintegration" and enabled "an inner integration, which before he had always sought outside himself." Shame broke up the coherence of the old self-structure, the one that had constructed the "world of sin"; and after the catastrophe a new self-and-world assembled itself. He passed through a gap between the worlds and found himself in the sacred cosmos.

Breakthrough into the kingdom of God was by no means a once-and-for-all achievement. The story of Francis's vainglory hints at the instability of the other world. For the moment he notices the poverty/shame gambit has succeeded, vainglory overtakes his consciousness and re-establishes the narcissistic defense. Francis is immediately drawn back into our world. There must sometimes have been quite a see-saw battle between mystic desire and narcissistic terror. Therefore, once he had discovered shame to be the portal into the other world, the new task of his sadhana had to be achieving *stability* in the sacred cosmos, acquiring the ability to stay there for longer and longer periods without interruption. In his eyes, his "sinfulness" was precisely the narcissistic impurity of his intentions, the fact that shame and grandiosity appeared at the slightest provocation and terminated the experiment. Francis is reported to have bemoaned this inconstancy in himself: "It seems to me that I am the greatest of sinners, for if God had treated any criminal with such great mercy, he would have been ten times more spiritual than I" (*2Celano*: 123).[11]

Life is potentially a dialogue with God. God treats him with great mercy—introduces him to lepers—and Francis performs an experiment, kisses a leper's hand and feels an exquisite joy (*L3Comps*: 11). If only he could dwell calmly in that joy without all the narcissistic rumbles. "Any criminal" would be "ten times more spiritual" because Francis regrets the countless lapses he has every day. This is not false humility. Because he constantly monitors his states of consciousness, he knows very well how many opportunities he has missed or terminated prematurely. When Francis speaks of sin, he does not refer to some crime he may have committed. Sin is lapsing narcissistically from the world in which he dialogues with God.

Sainthood and Heroism

A hero risks pain and possibly life itself to bring us some boon. Perhaps a life is saved or a foreign invader defeated. A mythic hero, like the Egyptian Osiris, dwelt on earth in an eternal era before time as we know it had come to exist. There he defeated his destructive evil twin, Set, and taught the ancestors of historical Egyptians the ways of agriculture and civilization, establishing a paradisal kingdom that served as a model for all temporal life to follow. Ordinary time began only after Osiris and his fellow gods had left this world forever.

The heroism of Francis of Assisi falls somewhere between that of the divine Osiris and that of the recent newspaper hero who saved someone from flames or undertow. According to Francis's early biographers, his life so closely followed the model of the God-Man, Jesus Christ, that he showed us what it means to live the life of Christianity's mythic hero—not in mythic time but right here in "ordinary time." After his death, hagiographic accounts elevated him and his sadhana of poverty to so lofty and mythic a sphere that Francis himself had become nearly a god, a superhero whose extraordinary gifts make his emulation a compelling ideal but not a realistic possibility.

In his heroism, Francis defeated no dragons, converted no Muslims, and unseated no rampaging knights. His battles were entirely of a different sort, as Bonaventure prayerfully reflects[12]:

> In the excess of his indescribable fervor, he did not even hesitate to kiss their ulcerous sores . . . He would expose himself to every kind of indignity, that he might bring his rebellious lower nature into subjection to the rule of the spirit; so he would gain complete control of himself and be at peace, once he had subdued the enemy that was part of his own nature (*MinLife*: I, 8).

The enemy, "his rebellious lower nature," the evil twin inside, the son of Pietro reassembled himself and the consensual world every time he found himself disturbed by a narcissistic emotion. Meanwhile, Brother Francis the religious hero and Friar Minor strove to live in the spiritual world and attempted to do so by cultivating peace. He would be "in control of himself" when he had overcome his sensitivity to narcissistic emotions, when he could face down anxiety, disgust, shame, vainglory, and the like, without losing his joyous participation in the kingdom of heaven. The utter imperturbability he sought was difficult—if not impossible—to sustain. Therefore, the sadhana of imperturbability consisted in further experiments in standing up to disturbing emotions. Catching a wave of disgust rising within, he kissed the leper's oozing sores while bathing and bandaging him. He remained on the look-out for emotions that attached him to our world in hopes of passing through them peacefully. He sought to draw the leper's sore and its pus into his ecstatic cosmos instead of having them stir up a narcissistic crisis to pull him back here.

Francis's heroic battle with his narcissistic sensitivity resembles the followers of Shiva who deliberately seek out the disturbing emotions of disgust, dread, and lust in order to transcend them. A female guru from the city of Varanasi, in the early twentieth century says, "To train the tiger one must be close to the tiger" (Battacharya, 1988: 325). The tiger is our overwhelming susceptibility to the narcissistic emotions. As long as we succumb, we remain in the world of every day. Shiva "teaches man to disregard human laws in order to discover divine laws" (Daniélou, 1992: 15). He wants us to embrace reality without illusions. Because the world of the public consensus is filled with pretense and hypocrisy, the ecstatic hero faces up to the turbulent emotions that drive these vices.

The nineteenth century Bengali saint, Ramakrishna, found himself liberated when he could no longer distinguish between the tastes of sandalwood paste and his own feces. In his ecstasy he passed peacefully through disgust. Consequently, his hold on the sacred world was imperturbable (Kripal, 1995: 268). Along the same lines, Alexandra David-Neel tells a story about a Tibetan guru who claimed that enlightenment occurs when one can roll "in impurity like a pig and fashion stars out of dog dung" (David-Neel, 1971: 7). Summarizing the significance of such reports, Eliade says, "Assimilating every kind of filth makes the mind capable of any and every meditation" (Eliade, 1969: 297). The meditation that brings the sacred world to presence only persists as long as Francis can remain undisturbed by any form of disgust, shame, or vainglory. The narcissistic emotions are his "dog dung," the shadow of his sainthood and the nearly "tantric" secret behind his techniques of ecstasy.

The Sadhana of Imperturbability

The German Franciscan scholar, Octavian Schmucki, lists eight examples from the early biographies that demonstrate Francis had "a zealously sensitive nature and a sensibility easily aroused" which prompted him to impetuous acts driven by overwhelming emotions (Schmucki, 1991: 113–118). These examples imply that Francis must have spent a good deal of his time teetering on the edge of narcissistic crisis:

- He cursed friars who dishonored holy religion by their evil deeds and example (*2Celano*: 156).
- He threatened a friar who blackened the reputation of another with severe punishment, involving humiliation and a beating at the hands of a friar known as "the Florentine pugilist" (*2Celano*: 182).
- He issued a peremptory command that the friars immediately leave the house of studies erected at Bologna (*2Celano*: 58).
- He flew into anger and began tearing down with his own hands a building constructed by the citizens of Assisi for yearly Franciscan chapter meetings (*2Celano*: 57).
- He was subject to frequent weeping for the sufferings of Christ and his mother (e.g., *2Celano*: 200).
- He often rose from prayer with his eyes red from weeping (*L3Comps*: 14).
- He refused to stop weeping when doctors urged him to do so in order to save the health of his eyes (*MajLife*: V, 8).
- He was subject to frequent and sudden transitions between the emotional poles of joy and sorrow, praise and compassion, and the like, a narcissistic symptom that Object Relations theorists call "splitting" and which Jung calls "*enantiodromia*" (e.g., *2Celano*: 127).

The kinds of incident listed above suggest an individual who delighted in his emotional life. This seems particularly true of the three items involving weeping—where it must be noted that the sufferings of Christ and his mother unquestionably belonged to the sacred cosmos. When the Bible stories had become that real and present for Francis, he had to have been in an ecstatic state. And since it was his object to live entirely in the kingdom of heaven as Jesus had, we can hardly be surprised that he found the sacrifice of his earthly sight a small price to pay for other-worldly vision.

Four of the eight items, however, involve outbursts of anger over incidents that imply a compromise with his sadhana of poverty and its goal of "leaving the world": owning buildings at Bologna and Assisi, and unworthy behavior on the part of some of his friars. These are outbursts of emotion that unquestionably held him in the consensual world, and which his own words condemn. For example, in "Admonition XI" to his friars, he says, "A religious lives a good life and avoids sin when he is never angry or disturbed at anything" (Habig, 1983: 82). And in a letter to an unknown superior of a Franciscan province who was so upset at the sinful behavior of one of his friars that he desired to give up his post and retire to a hermitage, Francis gives a good deal of advice which supports the sadhana of imperturbability but which he did not always follow himself. Above all, he tells the superior, he should not desire that the situation be any different than it is, nor expect it to change. Rather he should love the sinful friar despite all, and accept this trial as a more valuable spiritual exercise than retirement to a hermitage. The miscreant should receive nothing but mercy and forgiveness from his superior (Habig, 1983: 110f). In short, Francis recognized that the superior was confronted with a narcissistic challenge, and that to learn to deal with his frustration and disgust imperturbably—so that his "perfect joy" not be disturbed—that was the holy sadhana God had prepared for him.

It is hardly surprising that Francis sometimes—or even often— failed to live up to the standards he set himself. This, indeed, is why he calls himself "the greatest of sinners." The central point is that narcissism was more dangerous an issue for Francis than it is for many of us. He was often overwhelmed with emotion, which is why his choice of sadhana was so appropriate. He worked with what life gave him, his volatile nature, and sought not to suppress its volatility but to enter into those emotions and learn to pass through them imperturbably.

There is, for example, a story from late in his life where he again reveals that he has been disturbed by the sight of lepers. He asks Brother James not to offend the public by taking them out of the hospital where people would be sure to see them, and then is horrified at himself for injuring the lepers' feelings. He confesses this sin to Peter of Catanii, the Minister General of the Order, and asks Peter not to object to his own devised penance, which is to eat with the lepers from the same dish (*Perugia*: 22; *Mirror*: 58). Since people ate with their fingers in the thirteenth century, he was planning to eat blood and pus from the lepers' sores along with his food. He had proved unable to deal imperturbably with the disgusting sight of lepers, so he set himself a more harrowing experiment. He was determined to pass through his disgust in the state of perfect joy.

At the time of this incident, he had been devising experiments to humble his grandiosity and shame for nearly twenty years; and just like the rest of us, it was still a struggle for him. Clearly he had grasped that sainthood is not an achievement but always an on-going process. The sadhana of imperturbability functions here, as well. For it is significant that after twenty years of practice his continuing disgust at the sight of lepers does not provoke a narcissistic crisis over the failure of his sainthood project. The dialogue with God goes on. He patiently performs a new experiment in imperturbability.

Possibly the best indication that he had learned something permanent from this practice can be found in his changed relationship with "Brother Body"—formerly known as "Brother Ass." His early companions tell us that from the hour the wooden Christ spoke to him in the rundown chapel of San Damiano, "He mortified his body most harshly, not only when he was well, but also when he was ill . . . so much so, that on his deathbed he confessed to having sinned grievously against Brother Body" (*L3Comps*: 14). He seems to have learned that while his body is both "this lump of flesh,"[13] and the whole complex of issues that anchors him in the conventional world, it is also much more than that. It is the instrument by which he performs the experiments of his sadhana. Brother Body is the vehicle that carries him between the worlds. The body remains an adversary, but a respected one: a recalcitrant worthy opponent for his idealistic and ecstatic identity. The battle between these two—the light and dark twins of his being—comprises the very means of consciousness changing.

Francis's zeal in the raw, early days, his desire to disown his recalcitrant tendencies, caused him to see his body as the enemy. And his maturity is suggested by the fact that he "reproved his brothers when they were too harsh on themselves . . . binding up their wounds with the bandages of sane precepts and directions" (*L3Comps*: 59). Though he is sometimes reported to have worn a hairshirt in the early days, he forbade such traditional devices be used by his friars (*Perugia*: 2).

Even as "Brother Ass," however, his body was at least a tireless and plodding vehicle, a hard worker but a slow one. Thus after perhaps a dozen years of experiments in poverty, he had begun to grasp the fact that the slowness and plodding were not due merely to his lump of flesh. They had to do with the more volatile, narcissistic sector of his psyche, the likely origin of his holy aspirations. He had arrived at a position outside of traditional rules about what constitutes holiness. In his late advice to Brother Leo, he makes it clear that it is not biblical models, ecclesiastical prescriptions, or even Franciscan tradition that describes the path. Rather, the path is constructed anew in every moment through a dialogue with God: "In whatever way it seems best to you to praise the Lord God, to follow in His footsteps and His poverty, do this with the blessing of God and my obedience" (Armstrong & Brady, 1982: 48). "In whatever way seems best to you": there are no rules for all situations. The practitioner of poverty is conducting a dialogue with God. The right thing to do is learned anew in every moment.

FOUR

Intercourse with Lady Poverty

The clue to his [Francis's] asceticism and all the rest can best be found in the stories of lovers when they seemed to be rather like lunatics (G. K. Chesterton, 1957: 15).

ONE ISSUE MAY have left the attentive reader perplexed during our study of Francis's sadhana of poverty: what was the origin of that "passionate fervor" that led to everything else? We have often seen Francis in an altered state of consciousness: his stripping before the bishop, his intoxication with God while speaking French, the reveries that dreamed up his experiments in poverty, the ecstasies at prayer when God seemed to speak or send a vision, the perfect joy that moved him beyond all temporal sufferings, and his sense that it was God who led him among the lepers. In all these cases something was moving him that we cannot call "will-power" in any ordinary sense of the term. For Francis did not soberly choose any of these experiences. In all cases he was carried away by some force greater than and even alien to his conscious will. This is, in fact, the meaning of ecstasy: *ek-stasis* (Greek), to stand outside oneself. We are very much within our own personal identity when we deliberately choose a course of action and then soberly carry out our plans. All of this falls within the scope of the ego. But when it comes to being carried away by powerful emotions or into actions that seem strange to oneself, the ego is no longer in charge—even if it continues to observe. Then we must speak of unconscious forces.

Talk of "unconscious forces" does nothing to eliminate God from the picture; for when God acts upon us, guides us into understanding something, the all-powerful One has no option but to use our mental and physiological faculties. To approach us in any other way would lead to no change in consciousness at all and therefore no communication. Thus, to make us hear the divine voice, see a heavenly vision, or challenge our nausea reflex will be to use the imagination, emotional sensitivity, and physiology of our body-and-mind.

In one way or another, the biographers all recognize that a dialogue with God requires observation of one's own conscious states, and that the ego-alien or "unconscious" quality of an impulse, image, or emotion points to its possible divine origins. For example, in speaking of Francis's youthful vision of a house filled with armor, saddles, and the like, and his initial interpretation that he was to become a knight and join an expedition to Apulia, Thomas of Celano observes that Francis should have known that this interpretation was wrong: "for . . . his heart was not filled with his usual happiness over such things. He had to use some force on himself to carry out his designs and to complete the proposed journey" (*1 Celano*: 5).

Celano makes it clear that Francis's mature approach to discernment relied on two factors: (a) does a projected course of action fill me with my usual happiness, i.e., "perfect joy," and (b) does the energy for carrying out this plan draw me effortlessly along, or do I have to use will-power to force myself? When the energy seemed to come from elsewhere (God, the Holy Spirit, the unconscious) and Francis found himself carried along in joy, then he knew he was on the right path. His mature style of discernment, in other words, sought to distinguish ordinary states of consciousness that support the conventional world from the ecstatic states that assemble the sacred cosmos. It seems unfair, however, for Celano to fault a young Francis who had not yet learned how to "leave the world" for not knowing the principles of discernment that dawned on him later.

In his *First Life*, therefore, Celano supports our understanding of Francis's sadhana as rooted in an effective awareness of his own conscious states, but fails to answer the question that concerns us. What was it that first moved the Poverello?[14] What taught him that an ego-alien force could fill him with joy and accomplish far more than mere will-power? Possibly aware of this failing in his *First Life*, Celano adds details to the vision of the house filled with military gear in his *Second Life*. Now the house has become "a splendid palace" which is also the home of "a most beautiful bride" (*2Celano*: 6). *The Legend of the Three Companions* is in substantial agreement. There the vision of military gear sets Francis up to expect another sort of life than he had previously imagined. Immediately afterward he is elected "king of the revels" by his partying companions. Thus as he reaches the height of his youthful popularity, he is pondering a vision that suggests he may be on the wrong path. Very likely he could feel an impending narcissistic crisis. Finding himself increasingly disillusioned and emotionally detached from the partying, Francis stops singing and begins listening: "All of a sudden the Lord touched his heart, filling it with such surpassing sweetness that he could neither speak nor move." His companions, noting his distraction, ask if he is thinking of marrying, to which Francis replies, "You are right: I was thinking of wooing the noblest, richest, and most beautiful bride ever seen." The authors go on to interpret that bride as "the true form of religion . . . noble, rich, and beautiful in its poverty" (*L3Comps*: 7). No doubt they are right, for Lady Poverty is the true form of Francis's religious practice.

Nevertheless, the most arresting fact is that Celano and the three companions all choose the emotive reality of eros to account for Francis's leap out of profane life and into the sacred world. First his dreams bring up peculiar images of a new way of life which operate upon him semi-consciously, interrupting his everyday consciousness with doubt and an unspecifiable yearning. They teach him that the answers are to be found within, for that is where he first encounters the "surpassing sweetness" that becomes the ultimate criterion in his mystical discernment. It feels like wooing a bride.

The erotic emotions always seem to come from elsewhere to overwhelm the ego in "surpassing sweetness." It can be no surprise, therefore, that nearly all mystics in every tradition rely upon eros and analogies with romantic love to describe their relationship with the

Absolute. In the biographies of Francis, the guiding emotion of eros is personified as Lady Poverty, about whom Celano says: ". . . he gathered her to himself with chaste embraces and never for an hour did he allow himself not to be her husband. This, he would tell his sons, is the way to perfection . . ." (*2Celano*: 55). These words are amazingly similar to certain stories told about the Buddha:

> The sage Vasistha . . . enters the great country of China and sees the Buddha surrounded by a thousand mistresses in erotic ecstasy. The sage's surprise verges on indignation. . . . He approaches the Buddha and receives from his lips this unexpected lesson: "Women are gods, women are life, women are adornment. Be ever among women in thought" (Eliade, 1969: 264).

Holy Intercourse
The earliest biography of all depicts the pre-conversion Francis in the erotic images of the Canticle of Canticles from the Hebrew Bible:

> Francis began to go about in the streets and crossings of the city, relentlessly, like a persistent hunter, diligently seeking her whom his heart loved. He inquired of those standing about . . ., "Have you seen her whom my heart loves?" But this saying was hidden from them, as though it were in a foreign language (*LadyP*: 5).

The Canticle of Canticles, or Song of Solomon, has long been a controversial text in that its unabashed sexual imagery has seemed to require an explanation to make it acceptable to the orthodox who want to be reassured that eros and sexuality have no place in a chaste relationship with God. This is surely one reason Francis's contemporaries found him to be speaking a foreign language. Sex and poverty are not understood by the conventional world, as the following parallel from twentieth century Bengal ("The Mad Woman of Calcutta") makes clear:

About twenty years ago in a residential section of the city, people used to see a very young and beautiful woman stopping passers-by on the sidewalk in front of her house and asking them, "Where is Shyama Babu? Have you seen him? If you tell me where he is, I will go and fetch him." Her beloved was dead and she was still waiting for him, living from her love of him. And love had betrayed her. The passers-by played cruel tricks on her.

Then another phase began for her. She clung to young men as they were going by and said to them, "You are my Shyama Babu, you have come back." Since she was not a prostitute, these men drove her away and ill-treated her, even threw stones at her.

After several years, one of her neighbors who had known her in the past noticed her sitting all day long at the foot of the sacred tree of that district. She had aged but her face was radiant with joy. She recognized her neighbor. He asked her, "Have you found your Shyama?" "Yes," she replied with a lovely smile. "Look, there he is," and she pointed to her breast (McDaniel, 1989: 192).

According to June McDaniel's research in contemporary Bengal, divine madness, the state of being driven mad by love for God, appears indistinguishable from ordinary madness to those who live entirely in the conventional world. But for the initiated, the love of God (*bhava*) is just too much to be contained within the ordinary psyche. It bursts the seams of its vessel and pours out in symptoms of madness until bhava can prepare a "self" that is big enough to contain it. The story of the Mad Woman of Calcutta illustrates the theory and may shed some light on Francis; for during the intermediate stage of his life, between the heedlessness of his early days and the conversion that led to his discovery of the sadhana of poverty, his behavior appeared love-mad and his words unintelligible to his contemporaries in the consensual world.

Furthermore, this sort of erotic experience sheds a good deal of light on our question: What was the origin of that passionate fervor that impelled Francis? The biographers point to eros, and eros is at its best and worst when the beloved is unavailable. It is at its "best" fever pitch and "worst" potential for generating madness. When the beloved is as "unavailable" and yet unforgettable as God, the human lover is truly in a fix and liable to try almost anything. This, we have to think, is how the biographers explain to themselves Francis's passion. Indeed, it is not unlikely that several of them had a personal acquaintance with this sort of religious eros. Bonaventure surely had.

For those of us who want to learn from Francis's discoveries and guess what we can do to find the portal between our own empirical world and a sacred cosmos of transcending meaning, we may be as much distressed as relieved to encounter this erotic factor. Eros is surely a standard-issue resource, part of what our body-and-mind can do. It fills us with sufficient enthusiasm to make daring moves, even pledge our troth. And it gets us in trouble. Eros explains the leap into so improbable an enterprise as poverty. Strong enough to overcome terror, disgust, and shame, it is itself a reverser of values. When the biographies say Francis was constantly making love with Lady Poverty, they mean that what motivated his trading downward was an inexhaustible infatuation. He was in love with the practice of poverty, with everything that had to do with trading downward. Like the lover of an earthly damsel, he followed his arousal. He did and said whatever increased his intoxication.

The biography of Francis that most explicitly develops the theme of his love affair with Lady Poverty is entitled *The Holy Intercourse of St. Francis with Lady Poverty*.[15] The work reads as a medieval morality tale. After seeking Lady Poverty in the highways and byways, Francis learns that she dwells on a mountain top. He and his spiritual brothers go there, where so few have succeeded, though it is an easy and joyful climb for them. Lady Poverty retells biblical history, her close relationship with Adam in the Garden of Eden, the long periods of abandonment she has suffered, her close relationship with Jesus and his disciples, another period of being forgotten and despised, and then the advent of the remarkable friars that stand before her "in her nothingness." They invite her to come down from the mountain and dwell with them. She does and is astonished to find they have no possessions at all to offer her, just themselves and what the earth provides. The work ends with the celebration of a nuptial banquet and mystical union.

Portraits of Lady Poverty

There is a famous mural on the ceiling of the lower basilica in Assisi in which a very serious-minded Francis, in robe and tonsure, is being married by Christ himself in the traditional Byzantine guise of the Pantokrater, the "Power Behind It All," to Lady Poverty. The bride, who is at least five inches taller than the Poverello, wears a dress prominently ripped, patched, and girt with a knotted Franciscan rope. Her eyes are huge, almond-shaped, and severe, her nose long and straight, her mouth tight. She looks more suspicious of Francis than loving, and he looks like a good-hearted priest who has no idea what he is letting himself in for. Did the painter[16] get it wrong? Were not Francis and the tattered lady too intimate with one another to strike such poses? She was the beloved who carried him into the kingdom of heaven on waves of bliss. She was his co-conspirator, his intimate; the slightest thought of her brought him to a halt, stirred up his physiology, set him to contemplating deeds of spiritual valor and contriving experiments to realize them. We see none of this passion in the painted Francis, and no reason why that gaunt lady in patches could inspire any sort of fervor. We are a long way from the Magdalen ways of Brother Jacoba, or the bright determination of Lady Clare.

Still, there is substantial justification for portraying Lady Poverty in a chilling light, for many of the things said about her are not at all flattering. Upon meeting her, Francis and his companions say:

> [Christ] came to seek you in the lower parts of the world, you who were lying in the mud of the swamps, in the dark places and in the shadow of death. You were not a little odious to all living creatures and all fled from you; and, in so far as they could, they drove you away from them (*LadyP*: 17).

She resembles the half-human Kundry in Wagner's Opera, *Parsifal*: howling in her misery, drifting back and forth with matted hair between the Castle of the Grail and the polymorphous perversity of the underworld. We keep finding her asleep; but when she rises up, men flee. We fear she may entrap us and want to be far enough away to ensure our safety. Thus Francis's first task is to encourage his followers to join in his improbable search for so hideous a lover. Right at the beginning of the drama he says:

> Wonderful, Brothers, is the 'espousal with Poverty, and we may easily enjoy her embraces, for she has become as a widow among the peoples, vile and contemptible before all, this queen of virtues. There is no one in this whole region who will dare to cry out, no one who will oppose us, no one who will be able to forbid us with any right to associate with her. All her friends have despised her and are become her enemies. And when he had said these things, all began to walk together after the holy Francis (*LadyP*: 13).

This unattractive, despised, and fearsome female is reminiscent of one of Hinduism's ten Mahavidyas, goddesses of "great knowledge." All are sexually promiscuous, but favorite consorts of Shiva; and all are terrifying figures—Kali, "the black one," with her necklace of skulls being the most famous. They are all opponents of the conventional world and revered as specially capable of destroying the ego that keeps us here—precisely the purpose Poverty serves in Francis's sadhana. Most similar to Lady Poverty is Dhumavati, a widow sitting in an unhitched chariot, "a woman going nowhere, the ultimate symbol of all that is unlucky, unattractive, and inauspicious" (Kinsley, 1997: 182). But sometimes she is presented as attractive, in which case she embodies the most threatening of women in Hindu society, for widows are believed to be driven by unsatisfied sexual longings they have no reason to resist (*Ibid.*, 190). Thus Francis says Lady Poverty has become a widow, despised and contemptible. The friars may easily enjoy her embraces, for no one will oppose them. Like the Hindu widows, we may expect her to be more than grateful for the attention.

In another famous portrait, Francis has had a vision of a woman one night when he had been praying for hours and sleep had gradually overtaken him. "His holy soul was taken into the sanctuary of God and he saw in a dream" a woman with a head of gold, bosom and arms of silver, abdomen of crystal, and comprised of iron from the waist down. She was tall, delicate, symmetrical, and beautifully formed but wearing a soiled mantle. Brother Pacificus saw that woman as "the

SALE

EAST WEST CAFE
2323 SONOMA AVE
SANTA ROSA, CA 954050000
7075466142
TID:00000XY4

DATE: 01/21/06   TIME: 20:49

MERCHANT ID: XXXXXXXX1620995
MI XXXXXXXXXXXXX6617

INVOICE: 81036   ID: 1
APPROVAL CODE: 021431   SEQ: 036

FOOD/BEV/TAX

$ 14.68

TIP $_____

TOTAL $_____

THANK YOU
COME AGAIN

BOTTOM COPY-CUSTOMER

TOTAL   ¢ _____

TIP   ¢ _____

   ¢   17.88

FOOD/BEV/TAX

SAVE

beautiful soul of St. Francis." From top to bottom, he said, the substances she was made of represented contemplation, wisdom, sobriety, and perseverance. The mantle is "the despised little body with which his soul is covered." Others interpreted the woman as Lady Poverty. Francis refused to give an interpretation (*2Celano*: 82).

The fact that the vision resembles the famous dream of Nebuchadnezzar, interpreted by the prophet Daniel as an image of the gradual passing away of earthly glory (Daniel 2), means that the story may have arisen and been remembered as a kind of prediction of the loss of prestige Lady Poverty was to undergo as the papacy and the councils of the church wrapped an ecclesiastical cloak, turn-by-turn, around Francis's sadhana.

Possibly the most disturbing element of the vision is the cold inflexibility of a woman comprised of metal and stone. Only the soiled mantle is soft and potentially warm. But the Buddha had an "adamantine body," said to symbolize the penetrating unshakability of enlightenment. The Sanskrit word for "adamantine" is *vajra*, which also means diamond, lightning bolt, and phallus. Perhaps some of the brilliance of vajra is suggested by the crystal abdomen of Francis's consort. But Lady Poverty's impenetrable body is not purely of one sublime substance and not uniformly gleaming, for iron rusts. Her composite form strongly suggests the four ages of the world's degeneration when we start at the head and work downward from the golden age to the iron. On the other hand, if we read the four substances from bottom to top, we are reminded of a graded series of mystical states of consciousness much like a Hindu subtle body comprised of chakras. Progressive stages of erotic engagement with Lady Poverty can also be read upward, where novices would be capable of a pitted and rusty iron intercourse requiring "perseverance," and accomplished mystics would be golden.

In her jealousy and capacity for revenge, Lady Poverty is as cold and steely a character as the most brazen of unflappable widows. Her rival is Lady Avarice who insinuates herself into our best intentions "by taking the name Discretion" (*LadyP*: 39, 43). Again the monitoring of interior states is described. We make love with Lady Poverty— or whomever our heart draws us toward—because she takes us to the kingdom of heaven. Avarice, by contrast, is an earthly fascination who winks and sways her way before us, wearing the inauspicious costume of common sense, and meaning to trick us into retreating to conventional states of mind. Dame Poverty stiffens the moment discretion enters our considerations, replacing the sacred world of poverty with a mundane concern for comfort and safety. She was faithful to Adam only as long as he remained naked. The instant he fashioned a skirt of fig leaves, she slipped out the back way and erased his name from her memory *(LadyP*: 30). She is inflexible and jealous, but when she finds one as unalloyed as Christ, she becomes "a most tender lover . . . [and] clung to him all the more faithfully the more [she] saw him despised by all others" *(LadyP*: 20). Francis undoubtedly knew Lady Poverty both in her cold inflexibility and in her warm embraces; for sometimes he accused himself of being the most unworthy servant of God and at others was transported in divine intimacies.

The Sadhana of Arousal

As hard a lover as Lady Poverty was, *The Holy Intercourse* tells us Francis was "faint with love for her" *(LadyP*: 9). And she says of him and his companions, "I see only that you are cheerful and happy, overflowing with joy, replete with consolation, as though you expect everything to be given to you just as you wish" *(LadyP*: 59). In the fleshly sense she was an unattainable beloved, like the high-born lady to whom the dashing knight pledged himself. Because "the knight's lady is mysterious, distant, and gracious as the Virgin Mary herself" (Cantor, 1994: 353), he sanctified his life through a longing that remained unsullied by carnal enjoyment.

Although courtly love may sometimes have been a military affectation, it was also a gallant gesture, an erotic consecration, a religious attitude, and a technique of ecstasy. The first troubadour, William IX, Count of Poitier and Duke of Aquitaine, wrote songs to the "Unknown Lady" he dreamed about while riding his horse. She became an erotic, mystic queen whom he served with heart and soul. Burning to take on whatever difficulties and risks she had in store for him, he said that obedience to her was simultaneously perfect fidelity to himself. "Through her alone," he sang, "shall I be saved" (de Rougemont, 1956/72: 88).

The practitioners of courtly love were very much aware that longing is the experience that purifies love and makes it "true" and spiritual. Pursuit of the temporary pleasure of orgasm may disguise itself as "true love"; but once the body has been satisfied, we may discover that our partner has served her purpose and is no longer interesting for us. An entirely different experience of love becomes possible when our beloved is removed from us by such implacable factors as geographical distance and social status. Sometimes the knights exaggerated this distance by choosing ladies who were skilled in a tantalizing fickleness. They wanted to increase their state of arousal by setting up a condition of unrelieved longing. For when our beloved banishes us to a great distance and no other partner can attract our interest, the person through whom we once sought pleasure becomes the object of our longing.

Longing itself is a state of ecstasy. When we deeply long for someone, the conventional world in which each person is interchangeable with every other vanishes, and we enter a landscape in which one dazzling beloved glides gracefully by shedding golden light upon everything she passes. A "subtlety" begins to make itself felt in our attitude. When the object of sexual pleasure becomes the apple of our eye, our interest in pleasure has begun its transformation into true love; and the engine for this change is longing.

Lady Poverty lived on a mountain top so far away that few had heard of her, fewer still had any desire to seek her out, and nearly all who tried fell into "the abyss that lies all about them." Francis and his companions succeeded only because they were "so unencumbered, all their burdens cast away" *(LadyP:* 14). The friars found it a joyful, easy climb; for to ascend that lady's mountain is to practice the sadhana of poverty and to reverse all values. To practice perfect poverty and live in perfect joy is to be always climbing the mystic mountain toward the beloved. Every step of the way is sanctified by longing. Longing was the bridge between the deepest ecstasy Francis experienced in God's world and the arousal of body-and-mind he required in order to make the transit to that world.

Francis's love affair at a distance with Lady Poverty, we may say, was the unifying theme running through his days and nights, his habitual meditation. For every passionate lover thinks incessantly and exclusively of the beloved whose very existence transforms the world. Every cloud and tree, every shop front and paving stone, every woman with bony shoulders, every young girl laughing, every lock of steelgray hair, every golden ray of sunlight: there was nothing that did not bring his disheveled darling to mind. Therefore, every gambit Francis hatched in his reveries, every experiment in narcissism he trembled to consider, was a patched cloak thrown over a puddle for *her* tender foot to pass, a nosegay of roadside blossoms to cheer her.

> So that he might not offend even once that holy spouse, the servant of the Most High used to do this: if he was invited by lords and was to be honored with a more lavish table, he would first beg some scraps of bread from the houses of neighbors, and thus enriched by want, he would hasten to the table (*2Celano*: 72).

Here we see how the sadhana of arousal works. A lavish dinner challenges Francis's ability to remain imperturbably in his perfect joy. To eat rich food at a splendid table in the company of nobles might provide so much earthly stimulation as to compromise meditation on his Poverella. How can he manage this extravagant entertainment without losing his state of aroused longing for his beloved? Although eros visits the ordinary individual erratically, when it will, maybe rarely, Francis was rather effective in stabilizing his erotic consciousness. He fashioned a life around the timeless ecstasy of that yearning emotion. Every moment had an erotic charge and was filled with the fragrance of his beloved.

The lord's invitation challenged all this with the prospect of a leaden, over-fed forgetting. The shrill edge of narcissism scared him. Powerful people would—not exactly wrongly—be proclaiming him a saint. Would he become inflated with self-importance? Or shamed at recognizing how unworthy he was? The stability of his ecstatic world was about to be tested. Probably it was already slipping, for look how much concern was entangling him. He reinforced his hold on the kingdom of God by stirring up his longing with the most fundamental exercise in his repertoire: begging scraps of bread from the houses of neighbors. About to be at the pinnacle of society, he deliberately trolls the back alleys. Facing the threat of grandiosity, he reminds himself of shame.

Like the lover who writes his beloved a rambling, wish-you-were-here letter, Francis imaginatively hangs out for a while in haunts saturated with memories of the intimacies and pranks he has shared with his beloved. His longing for her stirs the emotions and hormones of his body-and-mind, and gradually the radiance she familiarly sheds upon the world is restored from its state of near-eclipse. The beginnings of narcissistic panic had dimmed her radiance, but begging restores it. Begging re-establishes his brotherhood with the "minor" citizens of the town, puts him back at the bottom of the social order, like the poor man of Nazareth, like Dame Poverty herself. In remembering the perfect joy they have shared, he recharges his ecstatic consciousness.

Clearly Francis loved begging. He treated it almost as recreation, for it was his simplest and original technique of ecstasy and at the same time his primary mode of intimacy with his raggedy spouse. The unknown Franciscan who wrote *The Holy Intercourse*—even if he had not known Francis personally—must have been initiated into the tradition that linked eros with poverty; for he has the lady of the mystic mountain say, "I am joined on earth with those who represent for me the image of him to whom I am espoused in heaven" (*LadyP*: 64). The beggar's longing for her is the gateway between the world of space-and-time and the eternal cosmos. Francis begs "alms for the love of God," in order to rouse his body-and-mind to a higher frequency. Just like a lover who becomes lost in his beloved, all sense of time eludes him when he begs with his lady. In moments like that, we no longer know which of us is the mover and which the moved. Does Lady Poverty do the begging, or does Francis?

The Veil of Layla
The peculiar thing about longing is that if we are intense and unwavering in our devotion for a long enough time, we begin to change from the inside out. Gradually we find ourselves, all unintentionally, making the gestures, thinking the thoughts, and saying the words that our shining one does, over and over in our memories and dreams. Our beloved's heart beats within us. No doubt this is what the Mad Woman of Calcutta meant when she pointed radiantly to her breast and said, "See, there he is." The Shyama Babu she spent her life longing for is no longer to be sought outside. He has prepared a "self" within her, where he dwells in erotic contentment just beneath her skin.

In one of the oldest and best loved legends of Islam, the hero announces precisely this discovery when he says, "I am but the veil that hides the face of Layla." Stories of the lovers Layla ("night") and Majnun ("madman") actually predate the prophet of Islam by centuries. The Persian poet Nizami collected them into an episodic novel-length poem right around the time Francis—thousands of miles to the West—was beginning to seek rundown chapels in which to pray. According to the story, Majnun is so out of touch with consensus reality through his longing for Layla, that everyone knows him for a madman, and her relatives keep her confined to her tent lest she run off with the ne'er-do-well. They live separate lives, Layla under guard and Majnun a ragged desert hermit who communicates with the animals like Francis and teaches them the nature of love. Eventually through their devoted longing, Layla and Majnun discover that the difference between them has vanished. She says, "Once I was Layla . . .now I am madder . . . than a thousand Majnuns" (Nizami, 1966: 145). He says:

> If you knew what it means to be a lover, you would realize that one only has to scratch him, and out falls his beloved. . . . The name [Majnun] is only the outer shell and I am this shell, I am the veil. The face underneath is hers (*Ibid.*, 125).

Francis and his friars appear to have made the same discovery in their love affair with Lady Poverty. Certainly Brother Pacificus implies as much when he sees the woman of gold, silver, crystal, and iron as Francis's soul while the others are sure she is his beloved. Even clearer, however, is a tale Thomas of Celano introduces as "something of doubtful interpretation but most certain as regards the fact." It was about six months before his death, and Francis was on his way to Siena with a doctor "deeply attached to the order" in hope of finding a cure for "his eye trouble."[17] He met three identical-looking women dressed in rags who bowed to him and said, "Welcome, Lady Poverty." Francis could not have been more pleased and begged some money from the doctor to give to the women. The doctor gave them money, which they accepted. But after the two men had gone on and turned back for a last look, they found the women had disappeared. Celano says,

"These were not women who had flown away more quickly than birds" (*2Celano*: 93).

The heart of the story is the "supernatural" evidence that Francis has been "scratched" and Lady Poverty has fallen out. Francis has become identical with his soul, and lives entirely on the subtle plane. He has truly become the veil that hides the face of his Layla. His body is now unmistakably the soiled mantle scarcely covering the silver bosom and crystal abdomen of his mediatrix.

This is a most peculiar story, as it depends so much upon accurate vision from a man who was virtually blind and had to wear a hood over his head in the daytime to save his eyes the pain caused by even feeble light. The three identical women are to be taken for angels and their greeting understood as a message directly from God. Thomas of Celano goes out of his way to vouch for the accuracy of the scene, but fails to tells us where he got the story. The biographers sometimes give us a series of dependable individuals going back to Francis himself or one of his closest companions when they wish to establish the veracity of an unlikely-seeming report.[18] If the story did come from Francis, the events must have taken place in a vision; for he considered his blindness to empirical events the result of a shrewd trade that had gained him visionary sight. Perhaps he "saw" those angelic poor women on the road to Siena and reported their message to the doctor. The distribution of coins would then be evidence for how such stories grew after the holy man's death. But if the story did stem from a vision of Francis, the ultimate confirmation that he had become identical with his lady would then be internal to Francis himself.

The Forest on Fire

Francis of Assisi presents the unusual picture of a celibate saint who pursued a distinctly erotic sadhana. His spouse was an internal woman, the image of his soul, to whom he made love by begging and otherwise trading downward. His wooing her turned those experiments in poverty into ecstatic episodes. His consciousness was in the sacred cosmos while his body-and-mind were here in space and time. When we imagine him traveling through the valleys of north Italy in an aroused state, it seems unlikely that he could have avoided erotic encounters with the women who crossed his path. This is not to suspect him of failure in his practice of celibacy or even of subtle flirtations. We might rather suspect something quite innocent, that when he begged or preached there was something charismatic in his eyes, his tone of voice, the way he carried himself, his other-worldly conviction, that many women found irresistible. Such at least is suggested by the story of Clare's conversion to a life of poverty: "He, God's huntsman, was minded to snatch this noble booty from the world and to offer it to his Master. And so he visited her and many times she visited him, coming forth from her home in secret with an intimate female friend" (de Robeck, 1980: 31).[19] At another time he is said to have looked into a well and seen "the true face of Sister Clare, and it is so pure and shining that all my doubts have vanished" (*Ibid.*, 63). Thus tradition holds that Clare, too, functioned as soul-image for Francis.

Clare apparently met him about five years after he left the world, around the same time he met Brother Jacoba. Clare was eighteen, Jacoba twenty-two, and Francis thirty. The two women were certainly of an age to be impressed with a charismatic and spiritual older man who had had time to develop a stability and wisdom in his sadhana. One tradition holds that Francis and Clare traveled together in the early days of her dedication to God, and it was only when Francis noticed that their association was beginning to inspire gossip that he insisted on their parting. This is another miracle tale, for it is said that Clare asked sorrowfully when they would meet again. It was winter, and Francis answered that they would meet "when the roses are again in bloom," whereupon the frosted juniper bushes immediately bloomed with roses (Bodo, 1984: 40f).

The sense of the story seems to be that even if they spend the rest of their lives apart, they are in another sense always together. Their souls are united—like Layla and Majnun, Tristan and Isolde, or the many pairs of lovers in medieval romances who reach a stage in their erotic union that can only be realized through their entering separate monasteries. A wife who sought Francis's counsel concerning her own spiritual aspirations and how they were thwarted by her carnal-minded husband, was advised to ask him to join her in her sadhana. He did so, and they converted their marriage from a fleshly to a spiritual affair and found great joy (*2Celano*: 38). These stories depict the ultimate spiritualization of love. Whether they gladly die together like Tristan and Isolde, the rosebushes on their graves embracing one another, or they live together radiantly but non-sexually, or their souls are so united in God that they no longer require their bodies to be in proximity—all are instances of the spiritualizing effect of faithful longing.

When this part of Francis's story was told, he and Clare seemed to have set the world on fire. According to the legend, Francis made a point of visiting Clare at San Damiano whenever his travels permitted him to stay in Assisi. On these occasions Clare never failed to invite Francis to stay for dinner, and he always refused. Eventually his companions interceded for Clare. Sharing a meal with her was the least he could do for such a holy woman who also happened to be "his little spiritual plant." At this, the impulsive practitioner of the sadhana of reversal extended an invitation to Clare: she should leave her cloister and come to his shabby headquarters, the tiny chapel of St. Mary of the Angels where many years before he had cut her hair and invested her with the robe of a Bride of Christ.

There was a social visit before dinner was spread on the ground, "as was his custom." Then Francis began to speak of the ecstatic world with such fervor that he altered the consciousness of them all. Everyone at the table was "rapt in God." Meanwhile, the people of Assisi and nearby towns thought the forest was on fire, and the men all rushed out to extinguish it:

> They found St. Francis with St. Clare and all the companions sitting around that very humble table, rapt in God by contemplation and invested with power from on high. Then they knew it had been a spiritual and not a material fire . . .
> . . .Later, after a long while, when St. Francis and St. Clare and the others came back to themselves, they felt so refreshed by spiritual food that they paid little or no attention to the material food (*Flowers*: 15).

Although this story comes from fourteenth-century Italy, it has many cross-cultural parallels: the thousand-year-long uninterrupted, non-ejaculatory love-making of Shiva and Parvati which threatens to consume the universe in fire; Isis and Osiris who had already begun making love in their mother's womb; and the phallic trickster stories of China, Japan, and Africa, in which violating sexual taboos in the right manner becomes a most dependable source of wisdom. The most interesting is a genre of Buddhist hagiography, e.g., the eleventh-century Tibetan story of the female saint, Machig Lapdron. After years of meditation and study, she is informed by a sort of angel[20] that she should take a certain sage as her mystic consort. She brings him home, and their union produces so much light that her landlady believes the house to be on fire and opens the door. "She saw nothing except a room full of light and red and white spheres of light . . . She was afraid and fell into a deep sleep" (Allione, 1986: 150–87).

Two extraordinarily accomplished mystics, a man and a woman, enter a God-centered erotic ecstasy much more powerfully together than alone. The disturbing reality of this mighty ecstasy leads uninitiated individuals naïvely to believe a dangerous fire has been started in the empirical world. The ecstasy is so factual that even the spiritually blind have their eyes opened. It is not simply that the uninitiated know something has happened without knowing what it is, rather some sort of spiritual change in consciousness has been induced. The would-be fire-fighters withdraw "with great consolation in their hearts and with holy edification," while the Tibetan landlady falls "into a deep sleep." Those who dwell in the conventional world are drawn part way into the ecstasy of the saints. The landlady's experience is much like ours. She is drawn out of ordinary consciousness well enough; but because she has no facility in mysticism, she simply goes unconscious. The friars felt the same draw, but already being accomplished mystics, they knew how to develop an ecstatic state and hold it steady.

FIVE

Ecstasy and the Sacred Cosmos

> True prayer is never an escape from self but a centering on
> God, whose face reveals to me my own true face, the face God
> is summoning forth from my deepest center (Murray Bodo,
> O.F.M., 1984: 37).

AN ECSTASY SO powerful that the uninitiated cannot avoid seeing
something spectacular, perhaps even frightening, is clearly a literary
device designed to compensate for what biographer and readers cannot easily know: the "internal" changes belonging to the private, subjective experience of the saint. The world over, therefore, powerful
experiences of unitive mysticism are represented in hagiography as
phenomena of unearthly light, sometimes mistaken for a dangerous
fire in the material world; and levitation, being lifted away from this
solid world and carried elsewhere; or the induction of an altered state
of consciousness in uninitiated observers, whereby they see what cannot normally be seen and bring back stories of miracles. Spectacular
scenes, such as the apparent conflagration generated by the mystical
eros between Francis and Clare or between Machig and her accomplished sage, are reserved for the most advanced of mystics; and their

occurrence represents the culmination of one or more lifetimes[21] of extraordinary success in one's sadhana. In Francis's case, there is only one incident more numinous than the forest-fire scene with Clare, namely the vision of the crucified seraph that accompanies the first appearance of the stigmata and marks the beginning of the end of his earthly life.

A hagiography that gives us a saintly model for our own lives— rather than an unattainable ideal of near godly dimensions—will be careful to provide some important intermediate steps to help us iden- tify with the religious hero and imagine the course of our own poten- tial sainthood. Therefore, however much the saints may be exalted above the rest of us by the hagiographers, and even when they show signs of their future greatness in adolescence or even childhood, there are always insights to be gained and errors to be corrected. Reading about these lessons in the saints' lives helps us to see the overlooked mystical possibilities in our own lives.

Mystics are experts in attending to their conscious states, a skill that naturally improves with experience. Their field of awareness broadens as they learn to take accurate note of more and more details. Better observation leads to their recognizing distractions that may draw them back into the conventional world. As they learn to avoid these pitfalls, they gain a certain mastery in stabilizing their ecstasies, remaining in the sacred world for longer and longer periods of time. Maturation in mysticism involves two seemingly contradictory skills: (a) becoming more receptive to the images and mood-changes that come from outside the ego, and (b) gaining more control over the psy- chic conditions that make such visions and raptures possible. The mystic has to be *active* in maintaining a state of aroused consciousness but *passive* in allowing that ecstasy to go where it will. The ecstatic cosmos has to appear of its own accord, but the mystic has to maintain the conditions that keep that cosmos stable.

Regarding Francis's maturation in mysticism, we know that he was plagued with a narcissistic vulnerability that he first tried to conceal behind a cheerful popularity. He devised a partying strategy and prob- ably succeeded for a time, but it must have been a shaky success. Evidently there were moments of panic or dread, warning him that a narcissistic crisis was about to make partying impossible. Perhaps it all began in a crisis of shame when he refused the beggar. Perhaps he had already been praying intensively for some weeks or months when that humiliating incident occurred. At the same time, some mysterious erotic component was pushing him forward to expand his periods of prayer and devise some experiments in poverty. Eros aroused Francis's consciousness, intimating that he was very close to a numinous union with the discarnate God to whom he prayed or with the Christ whose spouse he shared. Eros drew him on to try harder and dare more, for it enabled him to "taste" his goal and convinced him that success was certain.

The legends say Francis's successes began early and not necessarily through any "merit" of his own. From his point of view, an agent quite other than and even contrary to his ego lay behind those events. It was, for instance, the initiative of a divine agent that made the wooden Christ speak to him. Francis had done nothing to deserve it. Indeed, quite to the contrary he felt himself lost and tangled in sin. There is no justice or predictability in mysticism, for many exemplary men and women have spent their lives in faithful sadhana without hearing the voice of God or being aware of so specific a command as, "Repair my church." Mystics, indeed, are rather like athletes. The memorable performers have been given a favorable constitution and a series of fortunate opportunities. They themselves have responded with unremitting hard work.

The Lessons of Brother Bernard

Bernard of Quintavalle, a wealthy nobleman, became Francis's first disciple and remained a close companion for several years, until there were enough disciples that missionaries could be sent to distant regions and he became one of the first. His conversion is described most simply by Thomas of Celano:

> He had often given the blessed father hospitality, and, having had experience of his life and conduct and having been refreshed by the fragrance of his holiness, he conceived a fear and brought forth the spirit of salvation. He noticed that Francis would pray all night, sleeping but rarely, praising God and the glorious Virgin Mother of God, and he wondered and said: "In all truth, this man is from God." He hastened there-

fore to sell all his goods and gave the money to the poor . . .
(*1Celano*: 24).

Later accounts are more elaborate, describing how Bernard hid
himself while watching Francis at prayer or how Francis sobbed, "My
God and my All!" the whole night long (*Flowers*: 2). The point,
though, is that Francis impressed Bernard first by "his life and conduct." Apparently Francis came across as genuine, honest, consistent,
and dedicated. The missing piece for Bernard had to be that elusive
"internal evidence" the biographers struggled to describe. He knew
Francis talked earnestly about God, but what sort of private, internal
relationship did he have with the divine? By spying on Francis after he
had retired for the night, Bernard learned prayer was so important for
Francis that he willingly sacrificed sleep for it. This implied a powerful emotional connection with God. Indeed, staying up all night to be
with another is characteristic of lovers in the deepest intensity of their
fascination. The Muslim mystic Rumi, a contemporary of Francis,[22]
says of his own practice of spending the night in prayer:

> When I am with you, we stay up all night.
> When you're not here, I can't go to sleep.
> Praise God for these two insomnias!
> And the difference between them
> (Barks & Moyne, 1984: §36).

Only an emotion as compelling as eros can make the reversal of all
earthly values a matter of joy. Brother Bernard was converted when he
saw that Francis prayed not out of duty or as a means of self-denial but
joyfully out of love.

It was a most essential and fitting discovery for Bernard, because
he soon found himself to have a rare gift for achieving erotic states of
consciousness—or as the tradition names it, "contemplation."
Contemplation, sometimes called "infused contemplation," is that
state of religious ecstasy in which the meditator exerts no effort of will
but is rather gripped and carried along by a force perceived as wholly
other than the ego and, indeed, divine. Evelyn Underhill quotes Hugh
of St. Victor to illustrate the nature of contemplative ecstasy:

It is indeed thy Beloved who visits thee; but He comes in an invisible shape, He comes disguised, He comes incomprehensibly. He comes to touch thee, not to be seen of thee: to arouse thee, not to be comprehended of thee. He comes not to give Himself wholly, but to be tasted of thee: not to fulfill thy desire, but to lead upwards thy affection (Underhill, 1961: 245).

Hugh of St. Victor describes the interior experience of contemplation, something Bernard could not have guessed from observing Francis at prayer. He saw only that there must have been something as powerful as eros behind Francis's devotion, and Bernard began experimenting immediately. Legend tells us that the practice of poverty led him directly to ecstatic episodes: "Because his mind was utterly freed and detached from earthly matters, he used to soar to the heights of contemplation as a swallow flies up into the sky . . . (*Flowers*: 28). His gift for contemplation, it is said, exceeded that of Francis and soon taught the Poverello that there were higher states of ecstasy than his eros for the divine had yet revealed.

The Little Flowers of St. Francis makes this point emphatically in an anecdote that appears to come from the very earliest days of Francis's experiments in poverty.[23] Perhaps Bernard was still his only companion, and Francis was still not confident of his conscious states. Since neither of them had any training in prayer, they must often have compared notes as to how they approached their meditation exercises and what results they got, what it felt like to address God, and how one would know whether God responded. Perhaps the most basic question concerned what God was doing to them and what they might be doing to themselves. Puzzled by some such issue, Francis calls to Bernard three times, to talk to him, "a blind man," about God:

But Brother Bernard did not answer St. Francis and did not go to him because, as he was a contemplative, his consciousness was at that moment suspended and uplifted in God.

Brother Bernard had a remarkable ability to speak about God, as St. Francis had already experienced many times, and that was why he wanted very much to talk to him. So after a while he called to him a second time and a third time, repeating the same words: "Come and talk to this blind man." But Brother Bernard did not hear him at all and so he did not answer him or go to him. Therefore St. Francis went away, feeling rather disappointed, wondering and almost complaining within himself that Brother Bernard, though called by him three times, had not wanted to come to him (*Flowers*: 3).

In his disappointment, Francis began to pray, whereupon "a Voice came to him from God." His questioning had been the effort of his ego, but the voice came from elsewhere, and so compellingly that he had to believe it came from God. When it said that Bernard had been entirely rapt in God and therefore was "so unconscious of his surroundings that he did not hear at all," the voice was very likely speaking what Francis had already learned "subliminally." He probably "felt" in some way the altered state of Bernard's consciousness, much the way our everyday moods can be affected by a powerful anger, fear, or awe in our companions. If so, the voice was enunciating what Francis knew implicitly. God had already spoken silently to him through the psyche of Brother Bernard, and now was repeating that lesson in a verbal form, audible only to his inner ear.

Francis taught Bernard that prayer could be more enjoyable than sleep, and Bernard taught Francis that prayer could produce an ecstasy so profound as to cut off all sensory connection with the world of space and time. The biographers give us the impression it did not take long for Bernard to learn Francis's prayer of erotic longing and that once Francis's eyes were opened to the possibility of a trans-sensory ecstasy, he was soon as oblivious to the world as Bernard had been. Both styles of prayer are ecstatic, for in ecstasy the realities of an alternate cosmos are more present and compelling than those of the empirical world.

Prayer performed in a state of ecstasy is therefore wholly different from prayer in ordinary consciousness, where one recites traditional formulas or urgently implores God for relief from suffering. Our everyday prayers call out from the world of space and time, hoping for a receptive ear in a sacred cosmos we merely "believe in." Ecstatic prayer transports the mystic directly to the other world, where there is neither belief nor doubt. One is overwhelmingly convinced. In

ecstasy, the sacred is real, a matter of experience rather than of specu-
lation. Sometimes the mystic gains this certainty of the sacred without
losing orientation in space and time, as Francis did before his crucial
lesson from Bernard; and sometimes ecstasy takes the mystic into a
condition of sensory oblivion.

The Ecstatic Condition
When Francis, Clare, and the friars entered an ecstasy so powerful
that the uninitiated believed the forest to be on fire, the biographer
ends his account by saying that when they had all "come back to themselves," they felt so spiritually refreshed that they lost their appetites
for the material food sitting before them (*Flowers*: 15). In this way the
superiority of the sacred cosmos is declared to be a matter of experi-
ential fact. Anyone who visits it can no longer be satisfied with the
conventional world. The author of *The Little Flowers* gives us a feel for
what it was like to enter the landscape of ecstasy in a story about
Brother John of Alverna, a priest who was often overtaken with ecstasy while saying mass, precisely at the point of pronouncing the words
of consecration, "This is my body." The author of *Flowers* tells us that
at those moments John was so conscious of a heavenly throng sur-
rounding him that he could not keep his mind on the mass. One summer morning it went so far that he collapsed and had to be carried
away from the altar and remained unconscious and "cold like a corpse"
from dawn to mid-morning. This time, however, he brought back a
report of what he had experienced:

> And because he used to confide in me a great deal, by the
> grace of God he told me all about it.
>   And among other things he told me that before and while
> he was consecrating, his heart became liquefied like heated
> wax, and his body seemed to be without bones, so that he
> could not lift his arms or hands to make the Sign of the Cross
> over the host (*Flowers*: 53).

We can easily believe an account like this, for we have all been to
the fringes of such melting. Early in the morning, for instance, when
we have been dozing and waking for an hour or more, we may not be
too lethargic to *think* about moving one of our limbs. When we first

notice this whim, we assure ourselves that we have the power to lift an arm if we wish—we just prefer the languid feel of unhinged knees and elbows as we drift in and out of fragmentary dreams. Whether we know it or not, control over our voluntary muscles has nearly ceased. We are only a step away from complete torpor.

Our torpor drifts kaleidoscopically through all those random thoughts and dream fragments, but Brother John's melting begins in the heart. Something wholly other has taken charge of his attention, something powerfully erotic, for his heart melts. In our morning doze, we are scattered and lethargic, but there is nothing distracted about Brother John's lassitude, for he is in the presence of his Beloved. He is focused and alive on another plane, where he has no need of his body.

Francis also knew such states of oblivion. Probably the most famous episode comes from late in his life as he is traveling through Borgo San Sepolcro[24] while "suspended in such sweetness of contemplation" that he was oblivious of his surroundings. People thronged out to touch him and cut swatches from his clothing while he paid no more attention than a "lifeless corpse" (*2Celano*: 98). Most of the stories of his ecstasies, though, have a more conscious quality. Thomas of Celano gives them a flavor of interiority and hints at the techniques Francis used to cultivate ecstatic states of consciousness. In one anecdote from early in his communal life with the friars, Francis wishes to have some indication of what the future will bring for the community, so he seeks out a place to pray:

> [A]nd he persevered there for a long time with fear and trembling standing before the Lord of the whole earth, and he thought in the bitterness of his soul of the years he had spent wretchedly, frequently repeating this word: O God, be merciful to me a sinner. Little by little a certain unspeakable joy and very great sweetness began to flood his innermost heart. He began to stand aloof from himself, and as his feelings were checked and the darkness that had gathered in his heart because of his fear of sin dispelled, there was poured into him a certainty that all his sins had been forgiven and a confidence of his restoration to grace was given to him. He was then caught up above himself, and absorbed in a certain light; the

capacity of his mind was enlarged and he could see clearly what was to come to pass. When this sweetness finally passed, along with the light, renewed in spirit, he seem changed into another man (*1Celano*: 26).

Celano gives us four stages of consciousness changing. First, in ordinary consciousness, Francis recalls shameful aspects of his past and begs God's mercy. He deliberately enters this remorseful attitude by visualizing himself standing before "the Lord of the whole earth." At this point his world has already changed, for in the everyday world we never let our speculations about God interfere with our pragmatic concerns. Francis undermines the profane world by repeating the mantra, "O God, be merciful to me a sinner." Entering the bitterness of his soul, he is no longer in the conventional world but not yet in the ecstatic cosmos. Rather he has conjured up the kingdom of God and divine judgment to stir his emotions to a froth. This second state of consciousness is characterized by Francis's vivid awareness of his blindness and insignificance before a God who has every reason to punish him. In the third stage he "stands aloof from himself"—the very definition of ecstasy. Unspeakable joy and sweetness convince him that his sins are forgiven.

In the conventional world, sin and God are realities to which people sometimes give lip service. In the badlands of remorse, sin is an overwhelming reality that sets Francis at a painful distance from God. Ecstasy begins when an agency other than Francis's ego "pours" certainty and joy into him. These are the hallmarks of the kingdom of God. But there is still a higher state of ecstasy, when he is "caught up above himself and absorbed in a certain light." Francis enjoys a degree of divine union and also gains a vision of the future.

The Psychology of Ecstasy

This technique of ecstasy can be specified more clearly. At the outset, Francis deliberately changes his consciousness with an act of willpower and disciplined imagination. He places himself, vividly in his mind's eye, before the Lord of the whole earth—the loving creator he so frequently forgets, the just judge before whom he has every reason to tremble. By this willful means, he plunges as deeply as possible into

sorrow and remorse. His method at prayer, therefore, closely resembles the technique of ecstasy he employs in his poverty experiments.
He enters directly into the world- and self-fragmenting sphere of
shame and unworthiness lurking in his depths. He deliberately risks
falling into a narcissistic crisis by courting emotions that precipitate
panic reactions in most of us. But this is not quite self-punishment, for
Francis has found that the most direct route to the sacred cosmos runs
through the narcissistic emotions. Resolutely and heroically entering
the sphere of narcissism brings about a grand and marvelous reversal.
When Francis's misery and remorse reach their pinnacle of intensity,
he is suddenly flooded with sweetness.

His ego willfully invites the pain and surely hopes for relief. But
he cannot *cause* his own reversal into joy. His ego is not the agent but
rather the recipient of this grace. Someone or some force wholly other
than the ego effects the glorious reversal that brings Francis into
ecstatic consciousness. He calls that agency God, and we can hardly
say his theological interpretation of the inner experience is wrong. If
God is the agent, however, we still would like to know whether
Francis's ecstasy is some sort of miracle (i.e., a divine intervention that
bursts the seams of human psychology) or whether it demonstrates a
principle of human psychology that others may follow while hoping
for similar results.

Among the world's religions this sort of reversal is not unprecedented. For example, India and Tibet have long cultivated "wrathful"
gods and goddesses of dangerous, irascible temperament, bloodthirsty
and full of lust. These divine beings are the very embodiment of the
narcissistic emotions. To see one of them in a vision is to enter the
panic of a nightmare, yet they are prayed to and revered as liberators.
Shiva, his analogues and consorts, wield the sword that beheads us,
destroying the ego that maintains our life in the conventional world,
thus opening up the sacred cosmos which is always present, though
hidden behind our fascination with the profane world of survival, the
domain of space and time.

Parallels like this suggest a common human element. Francis's
mysticism and that of the Hindus describe themselves with different
theologies but share the same human body-and-mind. In other words,
Francis's sadhana does not induce miracles but rather exploits a principle of human psychology. The "blissful" gods lurk behind their

"wrathful" twins, and the God of perfect joy behind the strong right arm of a righteous Yahweh. The divine being that inspires terror and shame is closer to us than the God of sweetness and joy, just as our foolishness, stupidity, and rage are closer than our more admirable qualities. Worshippers of the "wrathful" divinities have found that awe in the face of the Holy can most directly be stirred up in the body-and-mind by cultivating the disturbing emotions of dread, terror, shame, and the like.

Narcissistic emotions tear open the closely knit fabric of the ego's world and let in something else. What pours or slithers in through the gaps of the conventionally constructed world is almost certain to frighten us, for we have been holding it at bay most of our lives through repression and artful self-deception. Francis deliberately exposes himself to that existential dread, having learned that the "wrathful" emotions march at the head of a column of narcissistic energies and that, once allowed in, those energies not only destroy the old world construction but make possible a numinous reconstruction. Francis bore the panicky dread of the temporal world's collapse in order to gain the "bliss" or perfect joy that pervades the kingdom of heaven.

Heinz Kohut's notion of "narcissistic energies" represents the emotions closely linked with existential dread as being chaotic and disorganized in a primitive or infantile condition and claims they can later be organized and channeled—even into the extraordinary accomplishments of a Winston Churchill or a Dietrich Bonhoeffer. The heroes of myth illustrate episodes in the lives of individuals who have learned to channel raw, disorganized narcissistic energy into deeds performed at a level of mythic significance, what Francis experiences as the divine/human interface (cf. Kohut, 1985). The experience of Francis of Assisi seems to demonstrate that under the right conditions we can channel a large enough "volume" of narcissistic energy to support a sacred cosmos. Deeds ostensibly performed on the dense plane of temporality are also occurring on the more subtle plane of ecstasy.

Deliberately stirring up narcissistic emotions is a potentially dangerous undertaking, for such disturbing emotions are associated with the flaw in our self-synthesis. Consequently, exposing ourselves to them can result in that temporary or even permanent breakdown of

self and world we call psychosis. Francis and his followers were sometimes, especially in the beginning, suspected of madness, dementia,
drunkenness, and the like (*L3Comps*: 34); and when they attempted to
preach in more distant territories, they were thought to be "wildmen
of the woods" and heretics (*L3Comps*: 37). They opposed the customs
of the day, reversed all the values of the conventional world. They
were unwashed, flea-bitten beggars[25] with above-average intelligence
who were intoxicated with God. They courted psychosis so as to enjoy
ecstasy. Since they spurned ordinary consciousness, it is no wonder
people sometimes ran from them and threw stones.

Those who live in the realm of such raw and chaotic emotions
without succumbing to mental derangement must be possessed of
superior coherence in their self-organization, for they have withstood
the flood and the undertow and come out stronger. The stuff of madness is not different from that of ecstasy. The difference is that the
madman lacks breadth, depth, coherence, and structure, while the
mystic's psyche is superior in its organization, flexibility, meaning, and
spontaneity. Narcissistic energy is what the European alchemists of
Francis's day called the alexipharmic, the poison that kills and heals. It
kills the mental functioning of the schizophrenic while it carries the
mystic through the eye of the needle and onto the landscape of ecstasy. It kills the conventional world and heals by introducing us to the
sacred cosmos.

The Sadhana of Ecstasy

We have just described the essence of Francis's sadhana of ecstasy: his
deliberate provocation of the narcissistic emotions so that the influx of
their terrible energy, unconsciously organized by his superior self-synthesis, could carry him out of the conventional world and into the
sacred cosmos. Our entire discussion, however, was based on a single
passage from Celano's "First Life" in which it is claimed that Francis
was performing a sort of "divination," trying to obtain a peek into the
future. By itself, this incident does not appear to be part of a daily
practice. There is, however, a great deal of evidence that Francis was
constantly cultivating an attitude of receptivity toward everything that
belongs to the world of religious ecstasy. For example, in his *Second
Life* Celano tells us that when Francis was traveling with his companions and "felt the breath of the divine spirit," he would deliberately fall

behind the others so as to take advantage of what he experienced as a gratuitous gift from God (*2Celano*: 6). In another place, he says these incidents left Francis "drunk, as it were, in spirit" (*1Celano*: 56). Bonaventure claims they often led to Francis entering a state of ecstasy so profound as to leave him insensible of his surroundings (*MajLife*: X, 2). The same biographer also says, "He never ceased trying to sharpen his spiritual vision with floods of tears" (*MinLife*: III, 3); and that at the memory of Christ's crucifixion, "He could scarcely contain his tears and sighs" (*MajLife*: I, 5).

Such passages let us know that Francis was always on the alert for opportunities to make a transit between the worlds, constantly felt himself in the presence of a God who might deign to let him feel "the breath of the divine spirit." Other passages inform us that as often as possible Francis deliberately stirred up his narcissistic emotions with the drama and choreography of an itinerant actor, though he sought to move himself alone, and not an audience of spectators. Indeed, he exerted every effort to remain unseen, unheard, and unaffected if anyone should happen upon him: "When the man of God was left alone and at peace, he would fill the groves with sighs, sprinkle the ground with tears, strike his breast with his fist and having found there a kind of secret hiding place, would converse with his Lord" (*MajLife*: X,4).

Although Francis's sadhana made use of unexpected opportunities to leave ordinary consciousness and enter ecstasy, his days were much more organized than this employment of the fortuitous might suggest. The unexpected opportunities belong to the *receptive* dimension of mystical practice. On the *active* side, Francis was constantly repeating to himself some of his favorite Bible verses in praise of God. One of the texts deemed most authentic in the brief collection of works ascribed to him is entitled "Praises to Be Said at All the Hours." There are eleven verses, the first five and last three praising aspects of the godhead and the middle three praising the God who is manifest in the created world. Francis recited these verses at each of the seven canonical "hours," when Catholic priests and monks recite or sing the "Holy Office" (Armstrong & Brady, 1982: 101f).

In addition to these, we know Francis recited a medley of favorite verses throughout the day, a practice that resembles rather closely the Hindu employment of *japa*, or recitation of one or more mantras, especially while counting them on strings of beads. Such recitation maintains the mind in an awareness of sacred things, expanding the context of our experience so that the empirical objects and events before us are contained within a larger and more significant sacred cosmos. Usually there is a rhythmic character to the recitation that, in itself, is conducive to altered states of consciousness; and when practiced constantly eventually becomes automatic. It seems as though the mantra recites itself within one, and our consciousness of being guided by an agency other than the ego becomes habitual. As a result, fortuitous opportunities to expand into the sacred cosmos are more easily recognized and taken advantage of.

Most of Francis's prayer-like writings, such as the "Canticle of Brother Sun," are rather brief and easily memorized so they can be recited silently or aloud at any time of the day or night. But his most ambitious work of written prayer, "The Office of the Passion," has a more comprehensive goal of consciousness-changing. For each of the seven canonical "hours," Francis has assembled a string of verses, mostly from the Bible, that serves as the foundation for a meditation on an aspect of the suffering, death, and resurrection of Christ. At bedtime one meditates on Christ captured in the Garden of Olives, at midnight on Christ before the high priest, at dawn on Christ before Pilate, at mid-morning on the scourging, at noon on the crucifixion, at mid-afternoon on Christ's death, and at evening on the resurrection (Armstrong & Brady, 1982: 80–98).

In "The Office of the Passion" Francis brings together two of the most effective aspects of his sadhana: his spontaneous tendency to fall into "tears and sighs" at every thought of Christ's suffering, and the japa-like constant repetition of verses that describe biblical history, the sacred cosmos, and the majesty of God. In the meditative design of his "Office," furthermore, the diurnal rhythm of the earth is conformed to the central mythic events of Christianity. Because every earthly day recapitulates the suffering, death, and resurrection of the God-Man, its hours are made transparent to the eternal cosmos where the divine drama never ceases. "The Office of the Passion" is the liturgical expression of Francis's daily sadhana, the formalized shape of his consciousness-changing, the door through which the eternal becomes visible in the everyday.

Thus it is clear that Francis worked constantly in his waking hours at deliberate exercises designed to keep the possibility of the sacred cosmos fresh in his mind. He silently recited verses from the Bible and his own compositions, sometimes singing them aloud in his joy. There can be no question that this Christian form of japa eventually resulted in those verses and formulas "reciting themselves" within him—just as the "Jesus Prayer" ("Lord Jesus Christ have mercy on me, a sinner") became automatic for the anonymous Russian "pilgrim."[26] These exercises placed Francis in a state of mind that was extraordinarily receptive to impressions coming from outside the ego. When he noticed such "movements of the spirit," he would turn his attention toward them and allow them to influence him, changing his consciousness. At other times he was even more active, deliberately provoking the narcissistic emotions so as to enter the psychological space where ecstasy might supervene. The sadhana of ecstasy, therefore, was the way of life by which Francis maintained himself at the fringes of ecstasy.

The Eternal Cosmos: What Francis Saw

Apart from the familiar vision of the seraph and several dreams that are too allegorical to be authentic reports, we learn very little of the visionary world Francis entered in his ecstasies. He was careful not to reveal such matters; for he knew his ecstatic states would inspire wonder and amazement in others, which could easily lead him into "vainglory," or narcissistic grandiosity. Therefore he did his best to hide the outer evidence of his ecstasies beneath his hood and to dissemble when hiding was impossible. What we do get, however, are a number of hints concerning the transparency of the temporal world through which the sacred cosmos is glimpsed. For example, *The Little Flowers* describes a scene in which Francis and Brother Masseo have gone into a town to beg for their dinner with the plan of meeting again at a prearranged spot beside a gurgling spring where there is a large stone on which to spread the scraps they have collected. All goes according to plan, and Francis announces his delight in words that reveal this humble earthly scene as glowing with divine significance:

> "That is what I consider a great treasure—where nothing has been prepared by human labor. But everything here has been supplied by Divine Providence, as is evident in the begged bread, the fine stone table, and the clear spring. Therefore, I

want us to pray to God that He may make us love with all our hearts the very noble treasure of holy poverty, which has God as provider" (*Flowers*: 13).

Begging is a holy occupation because it takes the ego out of the driver's seat and hands over the reins to God. It is an activity that reveals the entire world as God's gift: not just the fragments of food gathered from door to door, but a random flat rock that dozens of people pass by every day without noticing emerges as a table. No restaurant, no waiters, no cooks, just an unmediated divine providing. The flow of all things from God out of love for us all, creatures of every type, is revealed the moment one stops striving and becomes receptive. Francis's openness to the flow of creation makes him conscious of his ecology in a way that seems remarkably modern:

> He told the friar who cut and chopped wood for the fire that he must never cut down the whole tree, but remove branches in such a way that part of the tree remained intact, out of love for Christ, Who willed to accomplish our salvation on the wood of the cross.
>
> In the same way he told the friar who cared for the gardens not to cultivate all the ground for vegetables, but to set aside a plot to grow flowers to bloom in their season, out of love for Him Who is called The Rose on the plain and the Lily on the mountain slopes. . . .
>
> We who were with him have seen him take inward and outward delight in almost every creature, and when he handled or looked at them his spirit seemed to be in heaven rather than on earth (*Mirror*: 118).

In a similar passage, Thomas of Celano reports Francis wanting the tree cut so that "it might have hope of sprouting again," and the garden's border be left "undug" so that the natural grasses could "announce the beauty of the Father of all things." In winter, he set out honey and the best wines lest the bees "perish from want in the cold . . . He called all animals by the name brother" (*2Celano*: 165).

The central theme in all these prayerful activities is the perception
that the world of nature praises God constantly in every one of its
processes. The growth and flowering of its plants, the singing and
soaring of its birds, the bowing of its trees in the wind—all these
things bear witness to a creator who has left evidence of personal
authorship and active love in every being and event. Nature is the
world as God designed it, while the politics, planning for tomorrow,
and economic strife of the conventional world represents God's world
as distorted by our petty and short-sighted egos. The world is the perfect cathedral for ecstatic contemplation when we can see it as it is in
itself. It only becomes "temporal" and grossly "material" for those of
us—admittedly the majority—who are entangled in ego-centered
striving. We turn a cosmos which is naturally holy, the domain of
divine generosity, into a world that is merely conventional, the profane trading floor of acquisitions which are mine, not yours.

Francis expresses this cosmic mysticism nowhere more clearly
than in his famous "Canticle of Brother Sun." There are fourteen
verses, the first two and the last of which praise God simply for being
God. The rest of the verses are designed to align the heart and mind
of the worshipper with the forces and entities of the universe (vv. 3–9),
human beings (vv. 10–11), and death (vv. 11–13). The sixth verse is
typical for the cosmos-centered vision it articulates:

Praised be You, my Lord
through Brother Wind
and through the air,
cloudy and serene,
and every kind of weather
through which You give sustenance
to Your creatures
    (Armstrong & Brady, 1982: 39)

Francis is not praising God for having created the wind, air, and
weather, nor for having given them to us. Rather he takes note of and
affirms the fact that Brother Wind and his cohorts sustain the plants
and animals, the rivers, forests, and deserts of the earth. Let God be
praised *through* Brother Wind's sustaining. The interaction of nature's

forces constitutes the dumb and unconscious praising of the cosmos in all its complexity. In taking notice of and affirming it, Francis brings this cosmic praising to consciousness. His ecstasies summon the universe, not simply as home, and certainly not as resource, but as showcase of God's beauty, power, generosity, wisdom, and love. Brother Wind's blowing reveals the form of cosmic worship. Francis's ecstasy and his begging participate in that worship and make it conscious.

Pouring Out and Pouring Through

Francis's model was always the God-Man, Christ, the unique and ultimate instance for Christians, of divinity inhabiting the cosmos of space and time. Of utmost importance was the fact that, though Christ entered matter, trod the stony earth, and ate its bread to stay alive, he never became entangled in material concerns. He owned nothing, had no home, trusted his father in heaven to provide. Francis treasured his vision of the man, Jesus of Nazareth, robe in patches, feet dusty, preaching with happy heart the kingdom of heaven as an attainable state of consciousness. In his human identity, Jesus was a poor man. But Christ, the cosmic principle and divine hypostasis, was "metaphysically" poor. He had all power, the "fullness of Being," for he was God. But in a famous passage from Paul's letter to the Philippians, Christ poured all that divinity out, "emptied" himself of godhood, so as to become subject to the laws of biology and psychology like any other human:

> Be of the same mind as Christ Jesus
> who, as he already held the rank of God,
> did not think such equality with God a usurpation;
> yet he poured himself out
> taking up the rank of a slave.
> Fashioned in man's likeness,
> in form discerned to be a man,
> he further lowered himself
> in humble obedience
> to the point of death—
> to a death upon the cross.
> This is why God has lifted him on high,
> graced him with a name all names surpassing

so that at the name "Jesus"
each knee must bend, in heaven, on earth, and below,
each tongue agree that Jesus, the Christos, is Lord,
to add glory to God the Father (Phil 2: 5–11).[27]

Francis sought at all times to "be of the same mind as Christ Jesus," to cling to nothing, to be a slave in humble obedience to the divine will. But Francis had nothing to "pour out." Pouring out was what God did. For when Francis looked upon the world with his ecstasy-enhanced eyes, he saw nature, humanity, and every object and circumstance participating in the great pouring-out that is God's generosity. The rising sun freshens the breeze that sweeps clouds from the mountain and gathers them to produce rain to swell the dancing brooks. Everything leads into everything else in a grand out-pouring from God. Like the out-pouring Christ who became the humble carpenter, every being in nature gives away everything it has, taking what is fortuitously given only to give it away at the first opportunity, in an eternal round of sustaining generosity.

God is constantly pouring out, and nature is a complex process of pouring through. Francis's sadhana of poverty consciously takes up this pouring through and lives it prayerfully, in the same mind as Christ Jesus. Poverty, for Francis, was precisely that activity that most closely resembles God's world: clinging to nothing, joyfully giving everything away, allowing all things to pour through. Poverty is the most perfect alignment of oneself with the sacred cosmos, and Francis's ecstasies provided the refreshing vision whereby he saw that his begging and giving away participated in the great pouring-through which is the universe. In deliberately assisting the universal process of receiving from and giving to, he made himself a conscious partner in God's cosmic out-pouring.

SIX

Extraordinary Powers

[Francis] was then caught up above himself, and absorbed in a
certain light; the capacity of his mind was enlarged and he
could see clearly what was to come to pass. When this sweetness finally passed, along with the light, renewed in spirit, he
seemed changed into another man (*1 Celano*: 26).

I N THE LAST chapter we considered at length an ecstasy that
Francis deliberately induced by courting the narcissistic emotions. In
doing so, we pretty much ignored the reason the biographer gives for
Francis's having made this effort—namely his desire to enter the eternal cosmos in hopes of being able to "see clearly what was to come to
pass" for his religious order. We now take up the marvel of his success,
for he brought back a vision that consoled his few early friars. He saw
multitudes coming from every Christian country, choking the roads in
their zeal to put on the Franciscan habit and take up "holy obedience"
(*1 Celano*: 27). It was a vision of the future, a figurative and unspecific
illustration of success, despite some "bitter fruits" that could not be
avoided (*1 Celano*: 28). History seems to show that Francis was not mistaken in this ecstatic glimpse, for the religious order he founded

became a major force in church and society before the thirteenth century was out.

Admittedly, the Friars Minor were already quite numerous in 1226 when Thomas of Celano penned the story, and the truth of the alleged vision was already becoming obvious. Perhaps the vision itself was a gloss, innocently described by an enthusiastic disciple. Indeed, it is frequently impossible to distinguish legend from historical fact in the early biographies. Nevertheless, what seems fantastic by the standards of rational empiricism may well gain credibility when we move outside of thirteenth-century Italy and find strikingly similar claims made of the religious heroes of other traditions. Such parallels imply universal human capabilities. What was understood to be miraculous by Francis's Christian contemporaries has been described as a natural consequence of ecstatic experience by Hindus, Buddhists, Taoists, and Sufis.

Just as Francis's ecstasies parallel the heightened states of consciousness described in other cultures and religions, so also does his exercise of marvelous powers. Octavian Schmucki (1991: 143–57) categorizes some of them: predicting future events,[28] reading the secrets of others' hearts,[29] bilocation,[30] exorcisms and other "external" battles with the devil,[31] astounding and sudden healings,[32] and peculiar powers over animals.[33] With the exception of the exorcisms, these claims have vivid parallels in Ibn al-'Arabi's stories about the Sufi masters he studied with in Andalusia around the time Francis was beginning his experiments in poverty (Ibn 'Arabi, 1971).[34] In India, such "perfect powers" are called *siddhis*, which *The Encyclopedia of Eastern Philosophy and Religion* describes as follows:

> Among these occult powers are mind-reading, clairvoyance, materialization, levitation, making things invisible, and entering other bodies. All the great teachers have cautioned against the effort to achieve siddhis for their own sake, because such powers, even if they seem to be "supernatural," nevertheless belong entirely to the phenomenal realm and contribute nothing to one's realization of absolute truth, and because attachment to such abilities constitutes a serious obstacle in

the way of spiritual development (Fischer-Schreiber, *et. al.*, 1989).

Siddhis are human capabilities that "belong entirely to the phenomenal realm." Theoretically any of us could learn how to exercise them, though few of us do. Because they are rare and distinctively more interesting than such powers as walking, conversing, and dreaming, they inspire awe and admiration bordering on worship; or else the very thought of them disturbs us so much that we dismiss them as rational impossibilities. Some level of skepticism is surely appropriate, for the hagiographers have no doubt embellished some tales and told others for which they had questionable evidence. Francis's biographers are boundless in their admiration of him and determined to convince us that the saint was especially favored by God, who bent the laws of nature for him. From this point of view, ecstasy itself is miraculous, a state of "contemplation" that has been "infused" into the saint by a special act of God. From the Hindu perspective, however, siddhis are natural human capabilities that are "switched on" by the practice of ecstasy.

The Yoga-Sutra (IV, 1) says that the yogin's powers are a by-product of changes effected by faithful practice of one's sadhana. Some are passing and insignificant, but others are permanent and "spring from self-reliance" in those who are "free from desire." The document makes no attempt to explain how siddhis arise. Rather it is noted simply that they appear along the course of one's spiritual journey much as mountains and rivers reveal themselves to our ordinary senses (Feuerstein, 1990: 345). Hindu and Buddhist texts are far more concerned with the dangers of siddhis than with their marvels; for by getting caught up in amazement over them, in garnering applause by exercising them, or in speculating as to how they might arise, we are distracted from the goal of our spiritual journey, union with God.

It is not hard to imagine how these dangers manifest. As soon as we detect an instance of possible clairvoyance in ourselves, we begin to think there is something special, powerful, favored, or even "supernatural" about us. We identify these marvelous powers with our ego instead of recognizing that they come from elsewhere.[35] We can even become the worst sort of charlatan, the one who actually performs some of the wonders he advertises. In doing these things to win applause, we succumb to "vainglory." The narcissistic emotions, when they set us hectically to work for our own honor or advancement, pull us forcibly back into the conventional world and end our pursuit of the sacred cosmos.

That Francis's biographers were familiar with the danger of sid-dhis may be illustrated by Thomas of Celano's story of an exorcism (*1Celano*: 69). A man from the city of San Gemini intercedes with Francis on behalf of his wife who is "beset by a devil." "But because Francis preferred in his simplicity to be held in contempt rather than be praised by the world because of a demonstration of sanctity, he firmly refused to do this [exorcism]." Eventually, however, Francis gives in to the prayers of the citizens of San Gemini and his own friars.

> When the prayer was finished, blessed Francis went up to the woman, who was being miserably tormented and who was clamoring horribly, and, with the power of the Holy Spirit, he said: "In the name of the Lord Jesus Christ, I command you in holy obedience, evil spirit, to go out of her and never dare to hinder her again." He had hardly finished the words when the devil left that woman so very quickly and with such anger and racket that, because of the sudden healing of the woman and the very quick obedience of the devil, the holy father thought he perhaps had been deceived. He immediately left that place in shame, divine providence so arranging things that he would not be able to glory vainly in any way.

The next time he is in San Gemini, however, the woman comes running to thank him for successfully driving out her devil. Francis does his best to ignore her until Brother Elias prevails upon him to receive the happy woman.

Because he begins by praying and then speaks "with the power of the Holy Spirit," we know that the exorcism was accomplished in an ecstatic state of consciousness. We might have expected Celano to have gone on to praise Francis for his miraculous powers, but instead the entire story is overshadowed by Francis's struggle with narcissistic emotions. He appears to be more horrified at the danger of suffering a personal crisis of grandiosity than moved by charity to do the Christ-like work of alleviating misery. His behavior is close to one of the primary symptoms of "narcissistic personality disorder"—being so concerned about grandiosity as to lack normal human empathy.[36] The difference is that the narcissistic personality *seeks* grandiosity, while Francis *avoids* it; but both do so with no little anxiety. Celano interprets that anxious avoidance as a virtue, Francis's humility. His message is that the world needs such "demonstrations of sanctity," and Francis is called to perform them; but Francis responds reluctantly, for he finds his own salvation is always in the balance. His saintly way of life constantly skirts the pitfalls of narcissism. Experiments in poverty, healing, ecstasy—indeed all holy works—are accomplished only by facing a crisis of shame. Although Francis does not attribute the power to do these things to himself, but rather to the Holy Spirit, every success exposes him to the danger of grandiosity—either inspired by the applause of his well-meaning followers or by his own untamed narcissism.

The Psychological Reality of Siddhis

It looks as though deliberately placing oneself at the disposal of the Holy Spirit is a risky undertaking. For if that divine "indwelling" agency Christianity calls the Holy Spirit works through the unconscious of its human host, the human personality has to be open to the disturbing effects of unconscious forces. This precarious condition is precisely what we expect of those who live at the edge of narcissistic crisis. The flaw in their self-synthesis exposes them to a fragmentation of self and world that may result in the disaster of psychosis or the creative triumph of a new synthesis.

This condition has also been described in terms of "thin" or "porous" boundaries (Hartmann, 1991). According to this metaphor, the ego retains its distinctive "shape" by warding off psychic material that is alien to its everyday identity, as though by a membrane that encloses it. Clearly memories and intuitions can "permeate" the membrane, bringing in unconscious material from time to time, whereby it becomes obvious that an ideal "ego-membrane" will be "semi-permeable"—regular enough to support a sense of identity throughout changing psychological and environmental conditions and yet porous enough to permit novelty and inspiration. Looked at this way, a "flaw in the self-synthesis" and a "dangerous porosity of the ego-membrane" are two images that describe the same phenomenon: a habitual ego-identity which is threatened by an influx of unconscious material that may either overwhelm the individual in madness or bring about a "spiritual crisis," leading to a superior restructuring of the psyche.

When boundaries are "thin" or "porous," therefore, unconscious material more easily floods into consciousness, and the ego lacks definition with respect to the "inner world." At the same time, the ego loses definition in the face of the "outer world." We become more easily influenced by the people, opinions, and emotions in our environment. We lose our sense of having a stable social identity. It may even seem as though others get "inside" us and that we find ourselves "inside" them. Every therapist who has worked with psychotic, borderline, and narcissistic patients is aware of how psychologically "invasive" or "contaminating" they can be. They seem to have an uncanny knack for zeroing in on our weaknesses and secrets and speaking of them matter-of-factly and without doubt. It often appears they do not do these things intentionally; passing certainties simply come to mind and they give voice to them without much reflection. As a result, both we and the patients feel exposed, as though the normal boundaries that comfortably separate us from the world and one another have dissolved. Furthermore, reciprocal influences often result in the patient gaining a temporary sense of stability from the therapeutic encounter, while the therapist begins to feel strangely fragmented.

All of this seems to show that the ego's membrane forms a reliable boundary only in a relative sense. Some of us have a more stable ego-identity than others, but even the most stable ego can be undermined in situations of extreme danger and doubt. Indeed, what is more significant than an unchanging stability in our ego-identity would be flexibility, the capacity of the ego to restore itself after an experience of dissolution. That would really be the most effective solution to the ego's relationship with the unconscious: not to be isolated behind a "thick," "impermeable" membrane, but to be alternately receptive and standing firm as the ever-changing conditions of life require.

Without any sort of psychological theory to guide him, Francis seems to have discovered these facts and to have exploited them systematically. He was acutely aware that ego-stability was the essential starting point for a mystical life, for he shielded his novices from the dissolving shock of shame until their new ego-identity as begging friars had been sufficiently established. He also knew that too entrenched an ego-stability was the enemy of ecstatic consciousness, and therefore sent out his novices to beg as soon as they were able. He deliberately undermined their newly won stability through experiments in poverty and the sadhana of ecstasy, just as he deliberately exposed himself to narcissistic crises before "the Lord of the whole earth." The dissolving effects of his shame at being a forgetful and inconstant servant of God "thinned out" his ego's boundaries and made possible an influx of unconscious energies that autonomously structured the sacred cosmos of his ecstasies.

The ecstasies were valuable in their own right as rapturous reward, insight into the mythic foundations of human existence, erotic love affair with Lady Poverty, and subjective proof that a benevolent divine agent held the friar's precarious temporal identity in eternal and loving hands. But the transition from shame to ecstasy taught Francis something else. In that moment of thinned-out and dissolving boundaries, he discovered that other feats became possible, acts that seemed miraculous within the cultural assumptions of thirteenth-century Christian Italy but which have been located in the natural human sphere as siddhis since time immemorial by the Hindus.

What the Unconscious "Knows"

When Brother Giles is said to have had an ecstatic meeting with St. Louis, King of France (1214–1270), the others wanted to know why neither of them said anything. Giles answered that nothing needed to be said because, "The light of divine wisdom revealed our hearts to one another" (*Flowers*: 34). In other words, their boundaries were dissolved, and they met in that space of ecstatic openness that is well known to lovers, for eros is one of the most common dissolvers of the ego's membrane. This, too, would explain how Francis "peered into the secrets of hearts [and] knew things from which he was absent" (*2Celano*: 27). Both feats lie outside the bounds of sensory or deductive knowing. To know the secrets of others' hearts requires a mutual dissolving between oneself and another, as in the case of Brother Giles and St. Louis.

According to the claim that he "knew things from which he was absent," however, Francis is said to have had accurate and dependable access not only to the hearts of others but to impersonal events too distant for his fleshly eyes to see. He was clairvoyant: he entered imaginally into that distant place, and his vision of what was going on there was not wrong.[37] This is a much more difficult claim to make sense of unless we assume, with C. G. Jung, that the unconscious has "absolute knowledge." For if the unconscious is potentially in touch with the entire cosmos, it would only be necessary for Francis to "thin out" the membrane between the conscious and unconscious portions of his psyche to bring any empirical event at all into awareness—regardless the distance.

> You can never say with certainty whether what appears to be going on in the collective unconscious of a single individual is not also happening in other individuals or organisms or things or situations. When, for instance, the vision arose in Swedenborg's mind of a fire in Stockholm, there was a real fire raging there at the same time, without there being any demonstrable or even thinkable connection between the two [i.e., between the image of a fire in Swedenborg's mind and the empirical fire in the distant city]. . . . We must assume that there was a lowering of the threshold of consciousness which gave him access to "absolute knowledge." The fire in Stockholm was, in a sense, burning in him, too. For the unconscious psyche space and time seem to be relative . . . (Jung, 1955: ¶912).

In this passage Jung seems to imagine the collective unconscious as some sort of deep-bottomed container that holds a replica of the entire cosmos, from the nightly dreams of our spouse to the smallest speck of light in the world's most powerful telescope. This is not entirely a crazy idea. Indeed, it seemed self-evident to the ancient and medieval worlds that the human person or the human soul was a microcosm that corresponded in every detail to the macrocosm that contains Mt. Everest and the Milky Way. According to this perennial notion, each of us walks around with a perfect replica of the entire cosmos inside us, perfectly open to minute examination if our ego-membrane is thin enough. Recently physicists have come up with a similar image: the cosmos as a hologram or holomovement, in which each particle comprising it contains a picture of the whole. In articulating this vision, David Bohm says an "implicate order" lies behind the "explicate order" of the empirical world (Bohm, 1983). Rupert Sheldrake says we are guided by "morphic fields" that lie not so much inside us as all around us like energy fields (Sheldrake, 1995). If siddhis are human capabilities and not supernatural miracles, some theory such as these cannot be far off the mark.

Jung speaks of a "threshold of consciousness." The waters of the cosmic unconscious cannot pour into our awareness unless our "threshold" be "lowered." This is a variation on the metaphor of the thin or porous membrane. The thing that normally keeps our conscious identity and the shape of the world stable may be compared with the height of a dam, the impermeability of a membrane, or darning the flaw in our self-synthesis. We would be helplessly awash in that larger universe without the protection of a boundary, a structure, or a weave. Most of us cling to the security of that bulwark and never develop a knack for siddhis. A few, the mad, get washed out into the cosmic sea too soon and cannot find their way back. The accomplished, like Francis of Assisi, open and close that gap between the worlds as though it were a window sash.

Spiritual Influence

Clairvoyance, which includes imaginal access to distant times as well as places, differs from other marvelous powers by its impersonality. All the rest have something to do with mutual encounter (reading another's mind and heart) or mutual influence: levitation, bilocation, exorcisms and other sudden healings, entering other bodies, and influence over animals. Sometimes an observer reports what she "saw" (levitation, bilocation), making it clear that the observer's consciousness has been changed through an encounter with a saint in ecstasy. In other cases a recipient of the saint's influence makes a sudden change in behavior or manifests bodily or psychological changes (exorcisms, healings, entering others' bodies).

Spiritual influence from a saint in an ecstatic state of consciousness to a disciple becomes evident when the consciousness of the disciple has been changed. The practice of inducing a state of ecstasy as a teaching device is called *shaktipat* ("descent of power") in Hinduism. In Islam, where it is called "perfecting an imperfection," the shaikh places himself in the mystical state he wishes to induce and then, removing his "mantle," places it on the body of the disciple, transferring the ecstatic state at the same time (Wilson, 1993: 144). We know that Francis received Clare and his friars into religious life by investing them with a robe, but it appears that he usually did so without employing ecstasy. Nevertheless, although the Franciscans had no word for a transmission of ecstatic consciousness, the *concept* of shaktipat was not unknown to them. We have already seen how Francis is said to have influenced Bernard to practice ecstatic prayer, and how Bernard influenced Francis to deepen that ecstasy. *The Little Flowers of St. Francis* describes a more classic instance of shaktipat:

> And going out to his companion, all afire with love, [Francis] said forcefully: "Ah! Ah! Brother Masseo, give yourself to me!"
>
> And he said it three times. And Brother Masseo, greatly amazed at his fervor, threw himself into the holy Father's arms when he said for the third time: "Give yourself to me!"
>
> Then St. Francis, with his mouth wide open and repeating very loudly, "Ah! Ah! Ah!", by the power of the Holy Spirit lifted Brother Masseo up in the air with his breath and projected him forward the length of a long spear.
>
> Brother Masseo was completely astounded. And later he told his companions that he had experienced such spiritual consolation and sweetness in being raised up and projected by the breath of St. Francis that he did not recall ever having had such a great consolation in all his life (*Flowers*: 13).

This is resolutely an outsider's account, for we are given only two indications of shaktipat's influence on Brother Masseo: the cliché of levitation and the subsequent verbal report of great consolation and sweetness. Nevertheless, the description of Francis's state of mind when he embraced Masseo is highly erotic. Especially in view of the difficulties Christianity has had with erotic emotions and behavior, we may suspect this detail to be a fairly reliable element in the anecdote. For a morally questionable detail is likely to be preserved only when the tellers and hearers of the story require it to make psychological sense of the incident.

Other accounts of Francis practicing shaktipat are less extravagant but still retain the erotic component. For example, the abbot of a monastery in Perugia feels "unusual warmth and sweetness" and becomes "rapt in ecstasy and totally lost in God," when Francis prays for him (*MajLife*: X, 5). While spending the night out of doors in the snowy mountains, Francis keeps his companion comfortably warm through a single touch from his hand, heated by "the fire of divine love" (*MajLife*: XII, 7). Elsewhere, Bonaventure quotes Francis as saying, "If we were touched within by the flame of desire for our heavenly home, we would easily endure the exterior cold" (*MajLife*: V, 2).

Ecstasy and Physiology
The siddhi stories are about the power of ecstasy not only to introduce us to a sacred cosmos but to change our life in the empirical world as well. The chill of a snowy mountain pass is nothing to one like Francis who has mastered the techniques of ecstasy. Ecstasy either makes him insensible to the cold by transporting him to the sacred world where his five senses have been deadened or else stokes up the bodily furnace of his metabolism. If we are to believe Bonaventure, ecstasy very likely does both. For Francis not only "endures the exterior cold," he survives it in good health, without frostbite and without the deleterious effects of hypothermia. Ecstasy, therefore, is a temporary state of being outside one's (everyday) ego, where one not only contemplates an alternate cosmos but inhabits an alternate physiology.

Because we know that hand temperatures can be influenced by our emotional state as well as by hypnotic suggestion,[38] it does not seem unthinkable that the flame of heavenly eros could enable us to raise our body temperature. Indeed, there is a Scandinavian tradition in which shirtless men compete to see how quickly they can melt their way through a snow bank. Using psychological means alone, the contestants elevate their metabolism. Their altered state of consciousness is not merely mental and emotional, but physiological as well. These facts are well known in yoga, where ecstasy is said to generate a "heat" or "glow" called *tapas*: "From him that labored and practiced tapas were the three worlds created, earth, heaven, and the space between" (Fischer-Schreiber, 1989).[39] According to this sacred text of India, one heats oneself up through concentrated spiritual practice until one becomes hot enough that alternate worlds spring into being—or, more accurately, those pre-existent and "implicit" worlds unfold. The practitioner of yoga "broods" them with his metabolism like a hen. In the Katha Upanishad:

> Yama [the king of the dead] tells [the young Brahmin student] Naciketas the secret of the "fire that leads to heaven," a fire that can be referred either to a ritual fire or to a "mystical fire" produced by tapas. This fire is "the bridge to the supreme brahman"; the image of the bridge, which . . . generally signi-fies the initiatory passage from one mode of being to another (Eliade, 1969: 118).

Ecstasy, heat, and access to the sacred cosmos are all aspects of the same reality. Francis remains warm in the snowy mountain pass because the furnace of his metabolism has been engulfed in "the fire of divine love." He does not simply "desire his heavenly home," as Bonaventure puts it. He resides in that sacred cosmos. His body-and-mind are powerfully aroused and glowing with tapas. He does not merely "endure the exterior cold." He enjoys the tropical breezes of paradise, which are not merely imagined but supported by a real cor-poreal heat. Glowing with tapas under such circumstances would seem to require a tremendous expenditure of energy. Therefore, when he touches his shivering companion, a great power is transferred. Francis's altered state of consciousness acts like an energy field to wake the slumbering ecstatic potential in his companion. Shaktipat builds a fire in the friar's abdomen, and he enters an ecstasy that produces its own tapas.

* * *

Francis's most famous siddhi, his ability to communicate with and to influence animals, is perhaps the least amazing. For it is evident that animals, just like humans, become agitated or calmed through the influence of the individuals in their vicinity. In Hinduism, aspiring disciples are often advised to sit silently with a prospective guru to see what the teacher's presence does to their awareness. Only a guru who induces peacefulness ought to be trusted. Why then should not animals be attentive to our psychic states? It would surely be an evolutionary advantage in any species to be able to judge the dangerousness of an opponent by "sniffing" the emotional atmosphere. Humans can do it, though most of us have forgotten how. Very likely animals will have had fewer reasons to forget. If they "smell our fear," and our other emotions as well, they are likely to prefer to be near people who are deeply at peace with themselves, just as we humans are. Perhaps this is the ultimate significance of Francis's animals stories: they testify to a profound peace, depth, and solidity in the Poverello. The man who consistently employed the turbulent narcissistic emotions to enter ecstasy had become so much at one with himself, so well integrated, so flexible with his boundaries, that wolves, birds, crickets, and fish relinquished their fear and aggression while in his company—and, indeed, sought him out to enter that biblical paradise themselves, where the wolf lies down with the lamb.

SEVEN

Preaching and Improvisation

His habit was dirty, his appearance insignificant, his face not handsome, but God gave such power to his word that many families between whom were old feuds and spilled blood were induced to make peace. All felt such devotion and reverence for him that men and women precipitated themselves upon him and tried to tear off bits of his habit, or else to touch its hem (Thomas of Spalato, ca. 1220).[40]

F RANCIS TOOK TO preaching somewhat reluctantly; for he found "prayer"—what we might today call "meditation"—far more "spiritual" and rewarding. Preaching, he thought, would force him to choose between the sacred world and the everyday. "In prayer we address God, listen to him and dwell among the angels as if we were living an angelic life; in preaching we must think, see, say and hear human things, adapting ourselves to them as if we were living on a human level, for men and among men" (*MajLife*: XII, 1). Ecstasy transported him to the angelic world, while preaching would bring him back down to earth. There being no doubt where his preference lay, Francis had to remind himself that Christ had been a preacher, and had had far more to relinquish than a facility for ecstasy like his own. Christ had emptied himself of *divinity* to join us humans here on earth. If preaching the good news meant that much to Christ, Francis could hardly refuse. Therefore, when Clare and Sylvester rendered their verdict, that it was God's will that Francis preach: "He at once rose, girded himself, and without the slightest delay took to the roads. He went with such fervor to carry out the divine command and he ran along so swiftly that the hand of God seemed to be upon him, giving him new strength from heaven" (*MajLife*: XII, 3).

As soon as he became convinced God wanted him to preach, he threw himself into it with his characteristic enthusiasm. He discovered that "living on a human level, for men and among men" did not exclude the sacred cosmos. Indeed, the content of his ecstasies provided the material for his sermons and the fire with which to convey them. Sometimes he planned his sermons as carefully as any ordinary preacher and managed to deliver them as intended. But not infrequently he forgot what he wanted to say as soon as he found himself standing before an audience. He was used to shame, though, and frankly admitted his lapse just as he did while begging and praying:

> Without embarrassment he would confess to the people that he had thought of many things but could remember nothing at all of them; and suddenly he would be filled with such great eloquence that he would move the souls of the hearers to admiration. At times, however, knowing nothing to say, he would give a blessing and dismiss the people feeling that from this alone they had received a great sermon (*1Celano*: 72).

As always, his first thought was to try the familiar gambit of courting narcissistic emotions in hopes that with thinned-out boundaries and the worm of shame burrowing through his heart, he would open himself to ecstasy. Sometimes it worked. His mind was flooded with the light of the sacred cosmos and he would let the intoxication do the preaching. Sometimes the narcissism ploy failed. If so, there was no psychological reversal, and Francis would simply refuse to speak. Unless ecstasy was in charge, real preaching was impossible: "The preacher must first draw from secret prayers what he will later pour out in holy sermons; he must first grow hot within before he speaks words that are in themselves cold" (*2Celano*: 163). Francis had several techniques for "growing hot within." Sometimes he courted a narcissistic crisis; and sometimes, beginning softly and only gradually becoming vehement, he would sing himself into an ecstatic state of consciousness until "French words would pour from his lips" (Erickson, 1970: 68). Sometimes he became so intoxicated with God that he lost the power to speak and would gesticulate and dance "like a tumbler" (Englebert, 1979: 212). Preaching, whether in words, gestures, or pantomime, was always a by-product of ecstasy.

Spontaneous Improvisation

Francis surely "went out to preach," that is, planned to go to a certain place to talk about poverty, ecstasy, the religious way of life or whatever came to mind. Although what he finally said may have been a fortuitous expression of a momentary inspiration, his life as a preacher did not lack planning. He traveled as far as Syria to "convert the infidel." But every genuine instance of preaching was experienced by Francis and his audience as unique and spontaneous. He never knew when he would be inspired. Preaching, when it happened, was simply another instance of "pouring through." God took charge when he entered the angelic world; and when he preached, he recollected the sacred landscape of his ecstasy, where dancing and speaking were interchangeable means of expression. He was simply a conduit from God to his audience. Francis's ego observed and cooperated in this process but did not direct it. He knew a few techniques for encouraging ecstasy and for diminishing the distractions and narcissistic snags that might draw him back into the conventional world. But what happened when the portal to the sacred cosmos opened was always unexpected, always inspired awe. For entry into that world could only be gained when the ego relinquished control.

Francis could be as mysterious and unpredictable as the Buddha in frustrating the expectations of his audience so that they would hear what he had come to say. For example, there is a type of preaching story told of the Buddha in which he holds up a single flower in silence. For one of his disciples the gesture is more than eloquent, for it leads to his passing immediately into nirvana. People had gone to hear a famous person speak. They had looked for ideas, images, pas-

sionate urging, the feeling of being in the presence of a great and
saintly man. He gave them none of that, threw them back upon themselves. He had no wish to entertain or instruct. His goal was to transform his audience, to induce in them an experience that would reori-
ent their lives.

Francis's approach was not so different. For example, he reluctantly agreed to speak before the Lady Clare and her nuns, only
because the bishop insisted.[41] The women were excited to have a rare
chance to hear and see their beloved Father Francis, and that posed a
narcissistic dilemma for him. How could he present the word of God
so that the earnest ladies could really hear it and not be distracted by
their idealizing notions of his own presumed sainthood?

> Francis raised his eyes to heaven, where his heart always was,
> and began to pray to Christ. He then commanded ashes to be
> brought to him and he made a circle with them around him-
> self on the pavement and sprinkled the rest of them on his
> head. But when they waited for him to begin and the blessed
> father remained standing in silence, no small astonishment
> arose in their hearts. The saint then suddenly arose and to the
> amazement of the nuns recited the Miserere mei Deus [Psalm
> 50[42]] in place of a sermon. When he had finished, he quickly
> left. The servants of God were so filled with contrition
> because of the power of this symbolic sermon that their tears
> flowed in abundance and they could scarcely restrain their
> hands from inflicting punishment on themselves (*2Celano*:
> 207).

Francis solved the narcissistic problem of his own greatness getting in the way of his message with the familiar strategy of courting a
narcissistic crisis. He placed himself in the fullness of his sinnerhood,
before "the Lord of the whole earth." Celano implies this was not
exactly a calculated ploy. Francis began by deliberately altering his
consciousness, transporting himself "to heaven, where his heart always
was." The only part of this operation that Francis actively chose is the
shift of his attention from the empirical reality of his standing before
the admiring nuns to that non-ego place "where his heart always was,"

the ecstatic realm. He did not storm heaven with appeals for assistance but held himself open to any inspiration coming from the other side— from "Christ" or from "the unconscious center of his wholeness," or "self," depending upon one's preference. Only the shift in attention was deliberate. The inspiration that may or may not have followed would be entirely fortuitous and outside Francis's control. In this instance, inspiration was not long in coming, for he immediately pantomimed the narcissistic secret of his sadhana of ecstasy. Using theatrical props, he showed those women what it means to stand in one's shame before the Lord of the whole earth. He gave them no words of his own, nothing they could set aside as evidence of his genius or holiness. He spoke the words of the psalmist, David, when he was overwhelmed with guilt after seducing Bathsheba and deliberately sending her husband to certain death.

Francis redeemed an impossible situation. Those women saw themselves as his disciples. They justified their lives with the belief that they were following in the footsteps of a saint. Furthermore, his habitual avoidance of them only heightened their expectations. If he had delivered a brilliant and inspired sermon, the very thing to move the heart of a bishop or king, the Poor Clares would have heard it all as a marvelous performance by their own beloved Father Francis. It would all have been about the greatness of Francis (and themselves), while the word of God was lost. Francis believed himself incapable of solving this narcissistic conundrum. It was no matter for his ego to work out, but a crisis that could only be redeemed by a wiser agent than he.

Thinning out his ego-membrane, he entered ecstasy, and suddenly the impasse was resolved. Let the ladies gaze admiringly. Let them believe him full of holiness. Francis would enact the "emptying." Just as Christ poured out his divinity, so Francis poured out his sainthood. He became human, all the way down to the shame and guilt of King David, caught in his sin. Francis enacted for his respected but hopelessly infatuated sisters-in-Christ a collapse that is well-known to every mystic, the fall from sainthood to shame. Simultaneously, however, he enacted the shame-defying exercise that encourages ecstasy.

In meeting a narcissistic crisis with a wholly unanticipated act that defies social expectations, Francis illustrates the central technique of Ch'an Buddhism (Chinese Zen). Peter D. Hershock (1996) explains that the Ch'an practitioner achieves "liberation," not in solitary moments of ecstasy, but in social interaction when one is faced with a "narrative crisis" and transforms the situation by spontaneously improvising a response that alters the meaning of the interchange. By "narrative crisis," he means a breakdown in the story I tell myself about who I am. My identity and the meaning of my existence are called radically into question. I am on the verge of a narcissistic crisis. The social challenge that creates this dilemma, however, is my construction. It is only because Francis is vulnerable to feelings of grandiosity that he is intimidated by the high expectations of the nuns. The Ch'an solution for such a predicament is to do something that changes its meaning. By using the nun's idealizing projections against themselves, Francis so effectively shows his shame that both he and they forget his celebrity. In a moment framed by the blinding light of their glorifying expectations, he becomes sackcloth and ashes. They try to place a halo on his head, and he makes sure that its glow illuminates his grimy, flea-infested, and ash-besprinkled reality.

The primary training technique in Ch'an Buddhism (*fa ch'an*) is translated by Hershock as "dharma combat": "truth combat" or "sublime transcending combat."[43] It consists in the master's contriving one narrative crisis after another for the disciple, who has to learn how to transform those challenges, one by one, each by an act of spontaneous improvisation. Hershock imagines a jazz group in which the saxophone player injects an unexpected note, and the pianist takes it up as a revelatory notion and plays a new variation, a new "riff," on the old melody in such a way that the saxophonist's note takes on surprising significance. For example, the ninth century master, Lin-chi,[44] was expounding one of his favorite themes, "the true person of no rank" who acts from no fixed place and develops no predictable patterns of behavior. Suddenly a monk in the audience interrupted, demanding to know who exactly this person of no rank was. Lin-chi leapt off the dais, "began throttling the monk and demanded that he 'Speak! Speak!' When the monk failed to respond immediately, Lin-chi thrust him away, exclaiming, 'What kind of dry shit stick is this "true person of no rank"!'" (Hershock, 1996: 193).

This episode of dharma combat is begun by the obstreperous monk who interrupts Lin-chi's lecture. In doing so he creates a crisis for Lin-chi because the interruption comes from the "floor," from a man of lesser "rank," and exposes Lin-chi's position on the dais as a potential contradiction: "Here is a man with the highest imaginable rank lecturing us on having 'no rank.'" Francis's problem is quite similar, for obedience to his bishop places him in a pulpit where he is expected to instruct his female disciples in sainthood, a life of holiness. His lofty pedestal contradicts his message, the sadhana of poverty, trading downward, having "no rank," being a "minor." How can he preach "minority" from such an exalted dais?

Lin-chi responds to his crisis by leaping down from the dais and conducting himself as a highway robber, a man of the lowest rank. He reacts with spontaneous improvisation—completely unexpected and wholly out of character for a man of rank. In this manner he redeems the interruption and turns it into an opportunity to enact the thesis he has been expounding. Francis's solution is not so different. With all eyes ready for a display of his saintly grandeur, he opens himself to inspiration from the other side, and then decisively becomes a man of no rank, a shameful sinner standing before the Lord of the whole earth. Francis's improvisation, like Lin-chi's, inverts the meaning of rank so that the last becomes first and the first last.

In the third and final element of the story, Lin-chi throttles the obstreperous monk while shouting, "Speak! Speak!" He thereby announces that his second move in the drama requires a third—as though to say, "If you're going to challenge me to dharma combat, you had better be ready to reply." He disrupts the saucy personal narrative of the irreverent monk with a humiliating crisis. Furthermore by squeezing his throat while demanding he speak, Lin-chi assumes the shape of the poor fool's pride—which would have rendered him speechless even without fingers tightening on his throat. By contrast, Francis provokes a crisis of shame in the Lady Clare and her sisters without issuing a challenge to combat. The women are reduced to such despair over their unworthiness that "they could scarcely restrain their hands from inflicting punishment on themselves." Francis, whose aggression is never directed at anyone but himself, lays hands on no one. But by dramatizing his own crisis of shame, he inspires them to want to lay hands on themselves. Since they succeeded in "restraining their hands," we have to conclude Francis has led them to the verge of narcissistic crisis, the launching pad of ecstasy.

Theater of the Spirit

With the story of the gesture-sermon before the nuns, Thomas of
Celano invites us to admire Francis's humility and openness to divine
inspiration. If we also see the spontaneous improvisation of Ch'an
Buddhism, we do not diminish the Poverello's originality. Indeed the
Ch'an/Zen tradition is filled with flamboyant "characters" and outra-
geous ploys designed to open minds to a world quite other than the
one we all take for granted.[45] They are remembered for public acts that
were resolutely theatrical. Hershock notes that for the Buddhist, "the
world is irreducibly *dramatic*" (Hershock, 1996: 47). Evidently it was
also for Francis. Every human interchange was an opportunity for a
kind of preaching, and not always by going outside the community of
friars; for Francis loved to speak with them of God and to learn as
much as he could in exchange—as is shown in the anecdote about
Brother Bernard who was insensibly in ecstasy when Francis sought
his advice about prayer.

Preaching for Francis, however, was by no means always a matter
of proclaiming in words. From his initial stripping before the bishop
to his ordering himself laid out naked on the bare ground to die, his
life was marked by theatrical gestures drawn from the ecstatic cosmos
and occurring as spontaneous acts. Whether in ordinary consciousness or in ecstasy, Francis appeared to be aware of his audience.
Perhaps we should say that his audience somehow figured into the
largely unconscious "plans" that seem to lie behind his improvisations.
Theatricality so pervaded his mind that nearly everything he did was
suitable for the stage. When he sang himself into an ecstasy so that
"French words would pour from his lips," he was speaking the language of traveling theater troops. Despite his ecstasy—or perhaps
because of it—he became fluent in a language understood everywhere
but spoken nowhere, a language designed for communicating with
strangers, the language of the stage. When he sprinkled ashes on his
head before the nuns, he somehow knew—or something inside him
knew—what strings to pull with this particular audience. In the
thinned-out state of ecstasy, he knew the mind of his audience and
made the right moves every time.

But ecstasy was not Francis's only teacher. His dramatic sensibility was shaped by the popular entertainment of the Middle Ages, the
theater troops, jugglers, and troubadours that traveled from town to

town putting on displays both religious and secular. Even the church used the "special effects" technology of the day to recreate the miraculous and mythic events of doctrine in a theatrical manner. "In the miracle plays and mysteries staged for the populace, realism was the desired effect. A system of weights and pulleys resurrected Jesus from the tomb and lifted him to a ceiling of clouds" (Tuchman, 1978: 311).

A man as fun-loving, gregarious, and popular as Francis had been in his youth could not have been ignorant of these things. Therefore, what was worth remembering about his staging of "Christmas at Greccio" three years before his death was not that he may have been the first to construct a realistic crèche, complete with animals and hay, but rather that the quality of emotion and spiritual fervor he roused marked a new development in Christian spirituality. Celano emphasizes Francis's "sonorous" voice and how he "bleated" the word Bethlehem like a sheep, and savored the name Jesus or Child of Bethlehem as though their sweetness left a delicious taste upon his lips and tongue. The biographer describes a man "entranced" by God and the mysterious significance of God's becoming human. A man thoroughly absorbed, in a mild state of ecstasy.

Evidently his dramatically elaborate and heart-felt reflections on the birth of Jesus succeeded, for "a certain virtuous man" in the audience is said to have seen the doll that played the role of the infant Jesus awaken "as from a deep sleep" when Francis approached it. "This vision was not unfitting, for the Child Jesus had been forgotten in the hearts of many; but by the working of his grace, he was brought to life again through his servant St. Francis and stamped upon their fervent memory" (*1Celano*: 84–7).

Some of the most effective things that happen on stage are improvisatory. Some theatrical performances are almost entirely improvised, except that the doors open on time and the actors have signed their contracts months ago. When Francis sprinkled ashes on his head before the nuns, only the time and place of the meeting were known in advance. The pantomime itself was spontaneously improvised. On some occasions, however, everything organized itself by chance, and there was no planning at all. For instance, a story is told of Francis's first encounter with Pope Innocent III, when he sought approval for his way of life as a "Rule" for a religious order.[46] In his forthright manner, Francis simply ambushed the busy pontiff with his request. The

pope, seeing only his discourtesy and shabby appearance, told him to
go roll in a pigsty, which Francis—in fine dharma-combat fashion—
promptly did. Muddy from head to foot, he presented himself to the
pope a second time, saying, "Lord, I have done as you ordered; now, I
pray you, grant me what I ask of you." The pope was reportedly so
impressed that he read Francis's proposal and orally approved the
Order of Friars Minor (Frugoni, 1998: 79).

The fact that such stories are told of the Poverello shows that he
was remembered as a man of unpredictable moves and open to inspiration of a type wholly foreign to everyday expectations. Sometimes
he rolled in a pigsty without forethought, as though the impulse came
from somewhere quite alien to his ego. At other times, however, conscious plotting played a significant role. When he was ill, near the end
of his life, his friars exerted no little effort to provide him with a new
cloak, which he promptly gave to a beggar. Knowing the friars would
not allow the man to keep it, Francis handed it over on condition that
the beggar hold out for a handsome price—which, of course the friars
were forced to pay (*Mirror*: 31). In the same vein, he would beg for
furs in winter while warning his donor that they would never be
returned (*1Celano*: 76). He was thinking ahead to the horror his
wealthy benefactor would surely feel to see her fancy cloak dragging
through the gutter on the back of a beggar.

Reading Injured Hearts

Francis's craftiness in these stories suggests another dimension of his
preaching. He knew the greed, willfulness, and vanity of the human
heart because he had dared to examine the one he regularly bared
before the Lord of the whole earth. He knew how easy it is to slip into
a narcissistic crisis, as well as how to court and how to avoid such disturbing events. Like a hunter in the woods, Francis had trained himself to see things the rest of us pass over. Bent twigs and over-turned
leaves tell the hunter which animals have recently passed by. Similarly,
the proximity of narcissistic shivers round his self alerted Francis that
an intended course of action risked setting off a panic of shame or
grandiosity. Foreseeing the narcissistic blow his benefactress was likely to receive, therefore, he gave her fair warning.

It is likely he saw the process of begging for and then giving away
the furs as a complex operation. In the first place, it was his personal

spiritual exercise, his sadhana, actively to participate in the cosmic pouring-through that describes the relationship between the sacred cosmos and this one. Francis's awareness of this mythic significance made passing down the furs from the wealthy to the poor an act of cooperation with God. Secondly, with respect to the poor recipient of the furs, Francis was performing an act of love and mercy, showing the beggar that God cared enough to clothe him as he did the animals of the forest and the birds of the air. It was a preaching gesture: "Be less anxious about your daily needs. God will provide. See, he gives you this fur-lined cloak to keep you warm."

The benefactress was also not forgotten, the third aspect of passing down the furs. Because she would surely see her furs mistreated and be provoked into some sort of self-righteous outburst, Francis could see that she was about to fall into distinctly "unchristian" behavior. But this was no regrettable accident. On the contrary, it was a divinely ordained insult to the "vainglory" she would surely feel upon donating a valuable item to a saint. He saw her inclinations and warned her of the rage and shame to come—emotions that point to the gap between the worlds. The benefactress was a good woman; and Francis, the practitioner of improvisational preaching, wanted her to find what lies beyond conventional notions of goodness. People who donated furs were comfortable in the conventional world—a condition Francis knew very well. His father was a successful operator there, and Francis himself had found it quite a playground.

For complacent inhabitants of the everyday world the alleged existence of a sacred cosmos will surely be a matter of rumor, superstition, or shallow romanticism. Indeed, to grant its reality is to invite serious doubts about the self-sufficiency of the conventional world. Francis knew how that sort of complacency can be undermined. His own disgust at the sight of lepers, for instance, and then shame at realizing he was more interested in protecting himself than in easing their suffering had opened his eyes to a latent narcissistic crisis. He decided to court that crisis and use its energy to change his consciousness. He turned his fleeing heart around and embraced the oozing leper. Because he owed everything to that painful self-confrontation, he hoped that his benefactress might experience a similar reversal.

The benefactress participated with him in the cosmic pouring-through, though she still lacked the spiritual vision to appreciate its significance. She helped alleviate the suffering of a needy person, though she did not quite know that and may merely have known that she was offering tribute to a holy man. Beyond that, however, she had begun (again quite unconsciously) to court the narcissistic emotions. For when she becomes self-righteously angry at the sight of her filthy, bedraggled furs, perhaps shame over her materialism and possessiveness will follow. Shame is the gateway. If there is an overarching theme in all of Francis's preaching, it is to seduce others into experiencing what had changed him. For the complacent, there was no substitute for being led to the verge of a narcissistic crisis.

Those likely to fall into despair provoked a different preaching style. For example, a story is told of converting a band of three robbers near a town named Borgo San Sepolcro. The robbers made the first move in approaching a small hermitage of friars to beg for food. The brothers did not know how to respond. Some thought Christian charity required them to give generously to the beggars despite their being robbers, while others thought Christian morality demanded they refuse to support evil-doers (*Perugia*: 90). In the end, Brother Angelo drove them away in righteous anger (*Flowers*: 26).

When he heard of the incident, Francis disapproved. He insisted the friars seek those robbers out and spread a table cloth upon the ground for them, laid with recently begged bread and wine. They were then to apologize for their self-righteous behavior. Eventually, they were to offer the robbers a deal: if they will give up robbing for a living, the friars will supply their needs from the proceeds of their begging. The result of this careful wooing is that the robbers become remorseful for their lives of sin and convert. In the more extravagant version (*Flowers*) they take up the religious life and are received into the Order of Friars Minor by Francis himself. Two of them die young while the third lives on to become a gifted ecstatic.

In this story, the recipients of Francis's spiritual ministrations are in no danger of complacency about the goodness of their lives or the favor with which God might view them. What precarious peace of mind they enjoyed must have required a steady suppression of conscience. They were surely defensive of their self-respect and likely prone to violence when insulted. But they did come *begging* to the friars, suggesting they were either desperate or curious. A preacher like Francis was habitually on the lookout for evidence of vulnerability—

exposure to the narcissistic sector of the psyche—which would have been apparent in the desperation or curiosity that drove those robbers to beg.

Brother Angelo was not so subtle. His righteous anger reminded them of the shame they were trying to silence and stirred up their defenses. Angelo himself, in fact, was skirting the edge of a narcissistic crisis, for he was dangerously inflated with his religious principles. In his incipient grandiosity, his finger-shaking emphasized the differences between the pious friars and the godless robbers.

Francis took the opposite approach. By spreading a common table and apologizing, he moved carefully around their shame, much the way he managed the shame of his novices. He needed those men to preserve what self-respect they had if his message were to be heard, so he took the burden of injured pride upon himself. No condescending saint, he sat down with them as a fellow outlaw, saying in effect: "I'm just like you, I live on what I can extract from others. The only difference is I take only what is willingly given. It sits easy on the conscience. You might think it an awfully naïve survival plan, but I assure you it works very well. We'll prove it to you. If you'll give up your violent ways, my brothers and I will supply both you and us with all the food, drink, shelter, and clothing we need."

It is easy to imagine how the holy seduction was carried out. Once they began eating daily at the friars' table, the atmosphere of equality and mutual respect had to have made them uncomfortable that the friars were taking all the risks. Possibly one or more of them went out on begging expeditions with the friars, and surely they all began to wonder at how happy the friars seemed to be. It overturned their usual assumptions to see that a decline in disposable income should be accompanied by an increase in joy. Francis knew from the beginning that the sadhana of poverty exerted a seductive pull on anyone who managed to gain a taste of it. It is the reason his order grew so rapidly in so short a time. Living the life itself, he found, could be the most effective form of preaching.

EIGHT

Life on the Rivo Torto

> In beautiful things
> he saw Beauty itself
> and through his vestiges imprinted on Creation
> he followed his Beloved everywhere,
> making from all things a ladder
> by which he could climb up
> and embrace him who is utterly desirable (*MajLife*: IX, 1).

T HE EARLIEST DAYS of Franciscan communal life were fondly remembered in luminous images by the first companions (*L3Comps*: 55). At first they stayed in an abandoned, run-down hut by a stream whose serpentine course named it the "Tortuous River" (Rivo Torto). As the shack seemed to have no owner who might object, they made it their base of operations. They ate, slept, and prayed there, while making daily excursions to beg or hire themselves out as day-laborers. Francis wrote their names on the beams, partitioning the crowded space into imaginary monks' cells. Each brother had his own space and tried not to intrude on the privacy of those on either side. They valued solitary moments for prayer, and many stories recount ecstatic incidents that occurred in the primitive conditions that made those days so magical when recalled.

Rivo Torto describes a way of life—an ideal picture of how to live the sadhana of poverty. No one knew the owner of that hut. The friars happened onto it by good luck or divine plan, the sort of thing that just comes along when you see the cosmos as a great pouring-through. Aside from the fact that it sheltered them at night, it was worth nothing. No one had to stand guard when they went out to rebuild churches or to beg. It left them unburdened and free to go wherever life took them, guided only by their sadhana of trading downward. Because every experiment in poverty was a spontaneous improvisation, they had no idea where they would be going tomorrow, or even this afternoon. They meandered through their days, cutting as unpredictable and serpentine a path as the Rivo Torto itself.

In fact, they lost the hut at the second or third bend. One day a peasant simply drove his donkey in through the open doorway, and without taking the slightest notice of the robed men standing about, informed his donkey that this was just the place for the two of them. Francis recognized this intrusion as the next move in a cosmic pouring-through. There was no question of asking the peasant and his donkey to leave. Rather Francis and the friars would have to go elsewhere if they wished to maintain their semi-monastic style of life. The hut at Rivo Torto had given them a starting point, and they took its spirit with them when they moved on. Its serpentine life-style became the earliest model of Franciscan spirituality

Francis went begging to the bishop and to the abbot of the Monastery of St. Benedict of Mount Subasio at Assisi. The latter gave the friars his poorest chapel, St. Mary of the Angels, which had long been known as the Portiuncula or "Little Portion" (*Perugia*: 8). Francis was delighted with that humble name, for it described their life of poverty (*Mirror*: 55). They used it for their prayers and liturgy and built beside it a small hut for shelter (*L3Comps*: 32). A strict discipline was established there of silence, hard work, and prayer, and only those living a religious life were permitted to enter. In this way they tried to live up to the official name of their "mother-house," St. Mary of the Angels: "Those who dwelt in this place were occupied with the divine praises without interruption day and night, and fragrant with a wonderful odor, they led an angelic life" (*2Celano*: 19).

It appears to have been standard practice at the Portiuncula and most other early communities of friars to divide themselves in halves. One group would labor or beg, leaving the other free for uninterrupted contemplation. After a few days or weeks of this, they would trade assignments so that the workers could pray and the others work (e.g., *2Celano*: 178). Those who worked restored churches, cared for lepers, hired themselves out as day-laborers, or stayed home to care for the community. Francis's earliest companions paint a paradisal picture of those days, when their experiments in poverty were all new (*L3Comps*: 32–47). Their ragged appearance made people think they were wildmen, fools, heretics, or brigands so that they often went hungry and had to sleep out of doors when they strayed too far from the Portiuncula to make it back by nightfall. Despite their disreputable appearance, however, they steadily took in novices who became as zealous in prayer and as eager to trade downward as all the rest. "They were so deeply rooted in mutual love: each one humbly reverenced his brother as a father or mother; and those brothers who held some office, or were distinguished by some special gift appeared the most humble and unpretentious of all" (*L3Comps*: 42). They obeyed without question whoever had authority, for they saw it as frustrating their own ego and doing the will of God. When they inadvertently offended one another, they courted a crisis of shame in their apology. "Thus they banished all rancor from their midst and kept themselves in perfect charity" (*L3Comps*: 43).

Ecstasy and Community

Wherever a common enterprise sets a group of people apart from the rest of the world, the group is sure to develop a sense of community based in shared values and experiences. The early friars surely had that, and reinforced their isolation through flamboyantly counter-cultural behavior and dress. Outwardly cut off from the world about them, and sharing huts at Rivo Torto and the Portiuncula where the walls of their cubicles were imagined rather than solid, they shared experiences that only another friar could appreciate. Furthermore, their sadhana of poverty left them as dependent on one another as a band of primitive hunter-gatherers. Such extreme conditions had to lead to the development either of indestructible bonds of affection or of animosity. But tales of strife are nearly lacking from those paradisal early years—the tragic story of "John of the Hat" (Giovanni della Cappella, who insisted on wearing a hat rather than a cowl) being a rare reported instance of insubordination and apostasy. Thus the evidence seems strong that the earliest friars were, indeed, bound together in "perfect joy" (Englebert, 1979: 45).

The sadhana of poverty was surely the primary glue that held them together, as it was the starting point for everything they undertook and determined the daily conditions of their joint life. Clare, in the Rule she wrote for her nuns, repeatedly cites poverty itself as "the means by which union with God and with one another is achieved and maintained" (Armstrong & Brady, 1982: 181). By the simple practice of eschewing all ownership, they became wholly dependent on God's bounty as it revealed itself in the provisions begged for them by the friars. In their daily activities, they supported one another and partook of one another's support; but compared with the men, they were the half of the community that prayed while the others worked, and they saw themselves as living out "the Inner Life of God" on the empirical plane: "The sisters are seen as a means of salvation in manifesting the profound relationships that exist in the Inner Life of God" (*Ibid.*, 184).

What it meant for the disciples of Francis, male and female, to "manifest the Inner Life of God" is powerfully suggested in Clare's "Fourth Letter to Blessed Agnes of Prague." Agnes was a Franciscan nun Clare probably never met and rarely heard from. We have to think that Clare's words are not quite "personal," since she and Agnes hardly knew one another in any ordinary sense of the word. Consequently, the unmistakable erotic tone of the letter can only be an expression of the intense love that bound their community together. That is what they had in common, not hours of conversation but a common way of life based on the sadhana of poverty, with its familiar goals, frustrations, and mystical rewards.

> Let the tongue of the flesh be silent when I seek to express my love for you; and let the tongue of the Spirit speak because the love I have for you, O blessed daughter, can never be fully expressed by the tongue of the flesh, and even what I have written is an inadequate expression (Armstrong & Brady, 1982: 205–6).

The close relationship between the sacred cosmos they inhabited
and the communal love that united them is powerfully represented in
one of the last adventures to take place at Rivo Torto. Bonaventure
says Francis had gone into Assisi one Saturday to get ready to preach
in the cathedral the next morning (*MajLife*: IV, 4). The rest of the friars were at home on the sinuous river chanting "the Pater Noster, not
only at the appointed hours but at all hours." They were cultivating
"the fire of the Holy Spirit" and their minds were in the sacred cosmos, when suddenly they were visited by a fiery chariot which traveled
two or three times round the room while "a large globe of light rest-
ed above it, much like the sun, and it lit up the night":

> The watchers were dazed, and those who had been asleep
> were frightened; and they felt no less a lighting up of the heart
> than a lighting up of the body. Gathering together, they began
> to ask one another what it was; but by the strength and grace
> of that great light each one's conscience was revealed to the
> others. Finally they understood and knew that it was the soul
> of their holy father . . . (*1Celano*: 47).

The biographers go on from this incident to speak of the "miraculous" powers Francis had—how he had accurate visions of the future
and knew the hearts of his friars, even when separated by significant
distances, and how he visited his brothers in their dreams and admon-
ished them. Thomas of Celano is prompted to tell several stories to
demonstrate these powers, one in particular about a certain Brother
Riccerio who feared that both God and Francis despised him. Francis
came to know of this apparently by "psychic" means, that is knowledge
of the poor friar's plight emerged from Francis's unconscious, drawn
up, as the author believed, by the Holy Spirit. He therefore visits
Riccerio in visionary form and reassures him of his love: "Come to me
with confidence whenever you wish and talk with me with great familiarity" (*1Celano*: 50).

All of these stories are about intimacy, about how the walls we
erect around ourselves in the conventional world artificially isolate us
as "subjects" from a world of impenetrable and inherently alien
objects. Ecstasy has taught Francis and the friars that when those walls

dissolve they can read one another's hearts. The ego-membrane thins out, and none is ashamed to have his conscience exposed. Shame passes over into the joy of union. When a friar's conscience is bare, there is none of the social razzmatazz that all of us use in the conventional world to hide our intentions from ourselves as well as from others. We see that friar's "essential being," the real motives, along with all the indecisions and uncertainty. We see a flawed man, just like ourselves, in love with God and the sadhana of poverty, but also hesitant, imperfect, compromised.

Francis's friars saw one another's' flaws, all right. But they saw these things while in an ecstatic state of consciousness. They saw one another in the light of the sacred cosmos. Celano makes it clear the friars had been maintaining themselves in an altered state of consciousness for some time before the fiery chariot appeared. They had been chanting "Our Fathers" constantly, thinning out their ego-membrane, learning to become attentive to whatever inspiration might come their way. Very likely they were not in a "trance," if trance implies that the ecstatic world completely obliterates the everyday and seems to be the only universe there is. The friars were more likely in a state of "reverie," where the reality of the ecstatic cosmos exists side by side with that of the empirical world.[47] Their Pater Nosters were holding them on the lip of ecstasy's chasm, and they almost fell in when all of them saw at once the fiery chariot of the sun god, a rare appearance of a fragment of ancient Greek mythology before the Renaissance. From C. G. Jung's point of view, this would identify the experience as "archetypal," an encounter with the "self," the god within, the organizing principle of the psyche, just as the sun is the organizing principle of the solar system.

This vision unquestionably is a religious experience of great power sufficient to establish the priority of the sacred cosmos over that of the everyday. But it is clear, too, that the friars did not lose all touch with the empirical world, for they began to look to one another, to compare impressions, and then to see that they were meeting in an extraordinary space of interpenetration and intimacy. They were lit up themselves in body as well as in psyche: "no less a lighting up of the heart than . . . of the body." Their body-and-mind was aflame with the emotional heat of a sun that made their skin and bones transparent and they saw one another's essential being. In seeing one anothers' hearts, they unriddled the image of the sun god and saw that it was Francis. Francis had become the sun of their universe through the numinous example of his joyful practice of poverty. His being shed light on their lives and bound them together. His way of life symbolized the center of each of them, individually, and their communal center, collectively. He exemplified both "self" and "community"; and when these two quite distinct realities coincided, the merely personal and idiosyncratic disappeared. The friars saw beyond their superficial and accidental differences down to their essential being. They were the planets circling Francis's sun.

The Ultimate Lesson of Rivo Torto

Bonaventure says that all of these events occurred at about midnight on that fateful Saturday, and the friars were left alone for some time without Francis to interpret the experience for them. Bonaventure, of course, was born too late to have known Francis personally, and we have to suspect that he was reframing Celano's account to bring it in line with his own mystical theology. In particular, it is worthy of note that the episode bears some resemblance to the "transfiguration" of Jesus in the gospels of Matthew, Mark, and Luke, where the disciples in an altered state of consciousness see Jesus shining like the sun and accompanied by Moses and Elijah. Time is somehow lost, and then they are back in ordinary consciousness and Jesus is instructing them. In Bonaventure's account, Francis "rejoins his companions" at some indefinite point and begins to teach them:

> He began to probe their consciences, exhorting them to take courage from the wonderful vision they had seen. . . . As he continued to reveal secrets beyond the grasp of human understanding, the friars realized that the Spirit of God dwelt in his servant Francis so abundantly that they need have no hesitation in following his life and teaching (*MajLife*: IV, 4).

This account of Francis's exhortation probably reflects the way Bonaventure, Minister General of the Franciscan Order some thirty-five years after Francis's death, exhorted *his* friars.

According to the narrative, Francis begins with the ecstatic experience they have had and uses it to "probe their consciences." He wants to make them aware of what is going on in their minds and the role played by their vision of the sun's chariot, as well as their experience of union. These are the sorts of change in consciousness that belong to the mystical path they are following. Therefore, Francis goes on from the experience they have had to leave them hints of what still lies before them if they should continue to pursue such altered states. He reminds them that all mystical experiments are exercises in attending to the changes in one's own awareness, and by directing their attention to these things he strengthens their confidence so that "they need have no hesitation."

Hesitation is a well-chosen word, for it points to an experience Bonaventure, known as the "Seraphic Doctor" for his mystical erudition, must have encountered frequently in his own pursuit of ecstasy as well as in guiding his protégés. Anyone who has experimented with a reverie like that practiced at Rivo Torto will know that the most difficult question to answer is, where does it come from, this image or notion that floats before my mind's eye? He who hesitates is lost, for our ego raises reasonable objections, remembers precedents that threaten to take the edge off, notices how commonplace a certain thought is and declares it unworthy of the Holy Spirit. We keep asking ourselves: Have I made up this fiery chariot, or does it come to me in spite of myself? The problem of distinguishing ego-direction from spontaneous inspiration is certainly as old as the gospels, for Jesus is remembered to have told his disciples: "Do not be anxious how or what you are to answer or what you are to say; for the Holy Spirit will teach you in that very hour what you ought to say" (Luke 12: 11–12).

The author of *The Little Flowers of St. Francis* undoubtedly had that gospel verse in mind when he describes Francis's teaching practice with his friars (*Flowers*: 14). One by one he called upon his sons to, "Say about God whatever the Holy Spirit suggested to him." He ordered them all to be quiet and chose the first at random. As soon as it became clear that the earnest brother was speaking not from himself but "by the grace of God," Francis silenced him and called upon another. Each time he cut the speaker off as soon as his discourse became "profound," for it was not so much what was said that was important in this lesson but the ability to trust the ego-alien origin of inspiration, to speak without "hesitation" or the critical interference of the everyday ego.

Perhaps everyone has a handful of inspired moments in the course of a life. The regular practice of spontaneous improvisation, however, cannot be left entirely to chance. It occurs regularly only for those who have learned its discipline, and spent years in dharma combat. For Francis's teaching method surely resembles the Ch'an technique. The novice friar is put on the spot, confronted with a crisis of shame: stuttering and stammering before an audience waiting for the voice of God or, even worse, carrying on with a speech that everyone knows is rehearsed. Perhaps success would be worse: to speak inspired words and be so proud of ourselves that we make it into a technique, a "shtick," and never learn what inspiration is. For a community of God-centered men like these, nothing could be more important than gaining command of that ego-membrane, thinning and thickening it with intent. Whether they were going to preach or meditate, they had to have control of that.

This dharma-preaching exercise trained the friars to deal with humiliation. Novices were put in a position where they were sure to fail more often than succeed. Even Francis sometimes had to confess his blank-mindedness and leave the congregation with a simple bless-ing. Thus, it seems that the preacher who is determined to say noth-ing unless inspired is bound to be exposed to shame frequently and must learn to use it. Because shame's power to disturb is roughly pro-portional to its unfamiliarity, Francis sought out humiliating incidents and forced his friars to become acquainted with them. Surely these exercises were designed to "desensitize" the friars to the narcissistic emotions, but only as a first step. For the power of those emotions to thin out boundaries and push one through the gap into the ecstatic world was too valuable to be lost. Courting shame meant not just avoiding a fragmenting crisis but tolerating the panicky tension aroused and using its energy to step from one world into the next.

Such was precisely the result of the dharma-preaching episode described in *Flowers*:

While those holy simple men were . . . one after another speaking sweetly about God and spreading the perfume of divine grace, Our Lord Jesus Christ appeared among them in the form of a very handsome young man. And giving His blessing to all of them, He filled them with such sweet grace that St. Francis as well as all the others were rapt out of themselves, and lay on the ground like dead men, completely unconscious (*Flowers*: 14).

Here may be the ultimate experience of community and of loving one another "in God." Francis and his friars sensitized themselves to the divine source of inspiration. One by one they entered actively into the shame-courting psychological space where boundaries are thin and numinous notions and images cross over the line from the unconscious and are spoken in a kind of reverie that holds itself open to the other brown-robed men sitting in the shelter at Rivo Torto, as well as to the subtle plane that surprises and fascinates us with its ego-alien ideas. As more and more of them entered that space of communal ecstasy, they eventually were overcome with a vision from the ecstatic cosmos. They passed from reverie into trance where they perceived that their divine Lord was among them. It was a binding, erotic experience, the foundation of religious community.

Wandering the Serpentine Path

From Europe to Asia people were on the road in the thirteenth century. Sufis, Buddhists, Hindus, Cabalists, alchemists, Qalandars: all were wandering from one renowned teacher to the next, cross-pollinating their wisdom, preaching, conducting experiments, and instructing the uninitiated. Despite dangers of weather, terrain, and brigands, a great ferment of God-inspired movement was underway. In the West, it was not only friars who hit the road in their zeal, but students of all types. The "clergy," a category that included all students and professors, as well as monks, priests, nuns, and friars, were a privileged class and could easily support themselves with their literate skills or by begging. They sought the liberal arts in Paris, "the ancient writers at Orleans, medicine at Salernum, the black art at Toledo, and in no place decent manners" (Walsh, 1913: 55–6).

Perhaps the least mannerly of them all were the Qalandars of central Asia, a largely Islamic group with eclectic interests, whom Cyril

Glassé, in his *Concise Encyclopedia of Islam*, scorns as "a class of social outcasts, pariahs, and the mentally incompetent, who would more accurately be called unbelievers" (Glassé, 1989). By contrast, the contemporary scholar of Sufi movements, Peter Lamborn Wilson, has personally sought out the small bands of Qalandars that still wander today, and reports that a small but impressive minority of them, "are—by any fair standards—genuine mystics." He found some of the most convincing to be "devoted cannabis users"—an insult to responsible Sufis, who say that a true mystic cannot be a drug user. "A few were con-men and drug salesmen. The majority were amiable lazy wanderers of slight spiritual pretensions, very much like some of the young Westerners on the road in the Sixties" (Wilson, 1988: 202–3).

This probably describes the atmosphere Francis and his first followers entered in the early thirteenth century when they left the shelter at Rivo Torto or the Portiuncula and set out on the road to preach the new spiritual practices with which they had been experimenting. They took with them the serpentine spirit of pouring-through they had learned on the banks of the meandering river and wandered with only the most general notion of where they were going, prepared at all times to find new directions emanating from the will of God but manifest in the circumstances they encountered on the way. Wandering was as much an experimental undertaking as the sadhana of poverty, and was pursued just as joyfully.

These four brothers [Francis, Bernard, Giles, and Sylvester] were united in immense spiritual joy and gladness; but in order to advance their work, they separated.

Blessed Francis, taking with him Brother Giles, went into the Marches of Ancona, while the others took another direction. As they were journeying through the Marches, they rejoiced in the Lord, and Francis in a loud, clear voice sang the praise of God in French, glorifying and blessing the goodness of the Almighty. Their hearts indeed overflowed with joy, as though they had found the greatest treasure in the evangelical field of holy poverty; for her sake they gladly and freely considered all temporal things as dung (*L3Comps*: 32–3).

Nothing is said in these accounts of the friars' developing an entourage. No gaggle of optimistic youngsters with "slight spiritual pretensions," no husbands on the lam. The friars lived on the road as they had at home, admitting to their company only people who were already living the religious life. The spiritual air they breathed could only be sustained by fellow lovers cultivating the expectation that, at any moment, the empirical world can be ruptured by sacred reality. As they wandered, the friars tried to sustain that reverie they learned on the Rivo Torto, where the two worlds stood side-by-side. When inspired they spoke, otherwise they kept silence.

They disciplined their awareness while on the road; and whether walking or taking a rest, they focused their minds with their conversation. Either they spoke of God with one another, in a sort of dharma preaching; or else they recited the psalms and prayers of the holy office (matins, lauds, etc.). Their entire day was a liturgy of praise to God, very likely organized around early versions of Francis's "Office of the Passion," which made each hour a meditation on the parallel moment in Jesus' last day on earth. They determined above all to keep their minds on these details from the sacred cosmos and avoided all thought of planning their meals or their resting place for the night. Leaving such mundane concerns for God to figure out, they lived their intuition as much as possible and eschewed rational, ego-directed thought (*Flowers*: II)[48]

The biographers' reports suggest that Francis and his companions were not overly concerned about the destination of their travels, but enjoyed the wandering itself as a joyful spiritual exercise. Like lovers engaged in extended foreplay, their every move, gesture, and word was designed to heighten the arousal of their body-and-mind. They spoke of God joyfully, of how their consciousness had been changed, of the proximity of the sacred cosmos, and from time to time were so overcome that they had to kneel for a few moments to pray (*L3Comps*: 46). When they rounded a bend in the road and saw a crucifix in the distance, they immediately knelt down and said an Our Father. They entered every church and chapel they passed along their way and prayed: "We adore You, O Lord Jesus, here and in all the churches of the entire world; and we bless You because by Your holy Cross You have redeemed the world" (Englebert, 1979: 51–2). Francis sang, spontaneously in his joy, trying out verses that were eventually arranged into his famous "canticles" of praise.

The importance of wandering as a spiritual exercise in itself, a sadhana, is suggested by a few telling incidents. Brother Lucidus, for example, is remembered for attending to his state of mind when he found himself staying in a town for an extended period of time: "When he began to like a place, he would at once leave it, saying, 'Our home is not here, but in heaven'" (*Mirror*: 85). Thus, wandering was a way of preventing themselves from putting down roots of familiarity and comfort, roots that might attach them to an aspect of the empirical world and gradually seduce them out of their preference for the sacred cosmos. Wandering kept them detached from the mundane and courting ecstatic realities. As much as possible, they tried to share this mentality with those they met upon the way. For example, when invited to dine in the home of a well-to-do and pious Christian, they in their turn invited their host to join the lovers of Lady Poverty and go out begging before dinner. Many hosts are said to have been delighted to do so (*Perugia*: 60). Even Pope Gregory IX, who was driven from Rome by civil unrest, became a wandering anchorite to strengthen his spiritual resolve, and made a point of visiting the Lady Clare and the grave of Francis (*1Celano*: 122–3).

The Transparency of the Path

The full meaning of Francis's wandering cannot be appreciated without considering some details that might easily be misunderstood as "superstitious." For example, remembering that Jesus called himself the water of eternal life,[49] Francis made sure that when he washed his hands the rinse water would not fall in a place where it would be trampled underfoot; and he "walked on stones with fear and respect for Him who is called 'the Rock'"[50] (*Perugia*: 51). When he saw a worm on the road, he would pick it up and gently return it to the safety of the grass, as he recalled the words of Psalm 21, traditionally applied to Christ, "I am a worm and not a man" (*1Celano*: 80). When he found scraps of paper with writing on them, he would gather them with reverence, regardless of their language or former purpose, "because the letters are there out of which the most glorious name of the Lord God could be put together" (*1Celano*: 82)[51]

Francis had particular affection for Sister Lark, who dresses in earth tones and wears a pointed cowl like a friar and lives upon the grain she finds along the way, even in horse dung (*Perugia*: 10; *Mirror*: 113). Grains of wheat symbolize Christ and every Christian: "Unless a grain of wheat fall to the ground and die, it shall not have life" (John 12:24). Grains of mustard are emblematic of the kingdom of heaven, that specifically Christian state of mind that grows within one from a tiny point of certainty to a bush large enough to support the nests of birds (Matthew 13:31). As Francis and his friars wandered the roads of north Italy, they found it everywhere, this liberating, quasi-ecstatic state of mind, "the kingdom of heaven," especially in the "dung" of the material world. Everything plucked up on their travels—water, rocks, birds, wind, fields of grain, flowers, lambs, sun and moon, death—had a dual meaning for the friars. Water slaked their thirst and washed their hands before they broke their second-hand bread; but it was also the fluid of baptism, the fountain of living water springing into life eternal, the sea of Noah and Jonah, and the primal waters over which the Spirit of God hovered "in the beginning."

Nearly every object and event in the empirical world was susceptible to this mystic double vision. Everything was just the mundane thing it was, and simultaneously a radiant participant in the sacred cosmos. The friars lived in the thirteenth century as though Jesus of Nazareth had trod these very roads just last week. They remembered his every gesture and how their hearts burned within them when he broke into dharma preaching. Every object they encountered was a memento that he had lived. Everything participated in both worlds. Like us, the friars were quite capable of forgetting the ecstatic world. But they fought that tendency by cultivating prolonged states of reverie. When the two worlds are held steady, side by side, every stone, lark, and gurgle is transparent. For them, the imaginal fact that Jesus had passed this way last week, made every fig tree and bread loaf a gateway from the profane to the sacred.

Without having a word for it—other than "Rivo Torto"—Francis discovered the fundamental principle of all sacred wandering. In the Islamic tradition it is called *barzakh*, the Arabic word for "isthmus"— the narrow, serpentine strip of land that lies between the salt sea of the empirical world and the "sweet sea" of the sacred cosmos[52] The barzakh is the winding path where these two realities come together and every object and event encountered in ordinary consciousness has a sacred meaning that is immediately perceptible to any one of us whose mystical accomplishment has turned us into a "living barzakh":

> A Saint who spans the chasm of human and Divine knowledge may also be called a barzakh. Indeed man in general, in view of his conjunction of body and soul, matter and intellect, and above all individual and Divine consciousness, is also a barzakh. Because the barzakh touches the two worlds it is not only a separation, but also a bridge; thus it is very similar to the concept of man as pontifex [bridge-builder][53] (Glassé, 1989).

Francis's contemporary, the Spanish-born Sufi, Ibn al-'Arabi, who is known as "the Greatest Spiritual Master" (*ash-shaykh al-akbar*), began his spiritual wandering in the year 1194, when he was thirty. At a certain moment in the mosque at Tunis that year, he says he entered the barzakh and never left it. He called the intersection of the two worlds "God's Vast Earth," the "Realm of Symbols," and the "Earth of Reality" (Addas, 1993: 117).

> When I entered this Dwelling-Place, while staying in Tunis, I unconsciously let out a cry; not a single person heard it without losing consciousness. The women who were on the adjoining terraces fainted; some of them fell from the terraces into the courtyard, but in spite of the height they suffered no harm. I was the first to regain consciousness; we were in the course of performing the prayer behind the imam. I saw that everyone had collapsed, thunderstruck. After a while they recovered their own spirits and I asked them: "What happened to you?" They answered: "It's for you to tell us what happened to you! You let out such a cry that you have been the cause of what you see." I said to them: "By God, I had no idea I uttered a cry!" (*Ibid.*, 119).

We are reminded of the seeming forest fire the citizens of Assisi saw when Francis and Clare had their ecstatic dinner at the

Portiuncula. Both religious traditions assert that the mystical state of mind enjoyed by a saint may be so powerful as to cause visions and blackouts in nearby strangers. Like the fire fighters in the story of Francis and Clare, the laity in the mosque had only the dimmest notion of what has happened to them. We have to think a "shaktipat effect" pulled them out of ego-centered consciousness; and because they had no familiarity with non-ordinary states of awareness, they dropped into a kind of stupor or sleep. They failed to grasp what had happened to them, for the main events had occurred in the sacred world, which was unfamiliar and invisible to them. Their exclusive habitation was the salt sea of the empirical world, and when the sweet sea of God's Vast Earth drew near, they missed it. Like a sudden change in the composition of the air they breathed, the sweet sea knocked them out, and they never knew what hit them. The friars experimenting with dharma preaching also fell flat-on-their-backs asleep. But they did not awake bewildered. They knew where they had been. They were prepared for and familiar with ecstatic states of mind. When they fell into trance, they fell somewhere, and they came back with memories.

In that moment of crisis when Ibn al-'Arabi cried out and collapsed or when dharma preaching knocked Francis and the friars on their backs, there was a passing away followed by a return in which the one who returned was richer than the one who had passed away. Francis is often said to have become "a changed man" after an ecstatic episode. Sometimes he came back with a vision of the future or a new understanding of what he was about. Ibn al-'Arabi says that he came back to God's Vast Earth and never left it again. He lived constantly and without interruption in the Realm of Symbols, which was also the Earth of Reality. This turning point in his life was the beginning only of his geographical wandering. His mystical quest had already been long underway, as the reminiscences of his earlier career in Spain demonstrate quite well (Ibn al-'Arabi, 1971). He was already familiar with the reverie that holds two worlds side by side, with shaktipat, and with "sitting on the carpet of [God's] vision" (Ibn al-'Arabi, 1989: 26).

What made the dramatic passing-away-and-return in the mosque at Tunis unique was that the Realm of Symbols and the empirical world united for good. Ibn al-'Arabi no longer had to work to sustain a reverie in which the two worlds stood side by side. Rather, because the Realm of Symbols and the Earth of Reality were one and the same, every object and event in the empirical world was simultaneously a "symbol," a window onto the sacred cosmos. Before the passing-away, the sacred cosmos shimmered like the alternate worldview it was; after the return it had become solid. Ibn al-'Arabi no longer had to work to avoid *losing* the sacred cosmos, it was simply here every time he opened his eyes.

To mention just one other tradition, the nineteenth century Bengali saint Ramakrishna described the empirical world as a "Mansion of Fun" because its every object, event, aspect, and dimension participated simultaneously in the cosmos he had come to know through his ecstasies (Kripal, 1995: 176–9). With the possible exception of Bonaventure, who knew that Francis made "from all things a ladder to climb up and embrace" the divine Beloved, Francis's biographers may not have entered God's Vast Earth themselves. If so they never learned that the empirical world itself is the Realm of Symbols and Mansion of Fun. But even if they themselves never experienced this "solidification of the sacred," their stories leave us plenty of room to conclude that Francis entered that Earth of Reality. The numinosity and joy that radiates from those stories bespeak a wholehearted and repeatedly confirmed conviction that the sacred cosmos and the material world are aspects of one another. Scraps of paper with writing on them, worms stranded in the middle of the road, birds wearing cowls, the cosmic pouring-through of trading downward: all these things confirmed the sacred significance of the seemingly profane. Dharma preaching was a favorite technique for honing a friar's skill at "finding" the sacred cosmos at a moment's notice and then maintaining it by describing it to others. The sustained reverie that makes dharma preaching possible is the gateway to God's Vast Earth. Therefore, the passing-away-and-return the friars enjoyed at the end of the dharma-preaching experiment probably taught them the permanent lesson that Ibn al-'Arabi learned at Tunis: you can get to the point where the sacred world maintains itself, and is self-evidently present in every rock and tree.

When Francis and his friars took to the road, all these factors were in play. Dharma preaching maintained their joyful reverie and trained them to impart their message to those they met along the way.

Trading downward sustained the cosmic pouring-through that brought food and clothing from the wealthy to the poor. Tiny epiphanies were occasioned by every worm, lark, puddle, and horse-dropping. The communal love and joy of Rivo Torto was re-created at every turn of the serpentine path of their wandering. On the road in the early days of the Franciscan experiment, Francis knew he had discovered something essential about God and humanity, about this earth and the kingdom of heaven.

NINE

Crisis and Transcendence

The Little Brothers were to be poor in every sense of the word: poor in spirit, in possessions, in offices, and in learning. The kingdom of God within man was all they needed. The friars were, in accordance with the example of the apostolic church, to hold no property either individually or corporately. They were to live in abandoned churches, caves, or anywhere they could find shelter. Their physical labor was to earn them their keep, and if this did not suffice, they were to be mendicants. They were to obtain no privileges from the pope, and they were not to be ordained priests. They were not to seek learning because it was a snare and a distraction; to know that they should adore and serve God was enough (Cantor, 1994: 430).

IT WAS SHORTLY after moving from the Rivo Torto to the Portiuncula in 1209, that Francis found his band had grown to the exact number of Jesus' apostles. Francis was the twelfth, and the Christ of their constant awareness was in their midst as they set out for Rome in hopes of obtaining official recognition for their downward-trading lifestyle as the foundation for a religious order (Frugoni, 1998: 76–7). Experience had already shown them that they needed papal approval in order to defend themselves against suspicions of heresy. Anti-clericalism had been rampant in Europe for two or three generations (Cantor, 1994: 385), and deservedly so, as many of the clergy were uneducated and careless. Francis took a middle position. Unlike most of the heretic groups, he supported the priesthood as an institution; and instead of condemning slack and unspiritual priests, he hoped to educate and inspire them. He sent his friars with brooms to sweep out neglected churches and urge local priests to keep their altars clean (*Mirror*: 56). He also tried to supply wafer irons to make proper communion hosts and clean pyxes in which to carry them (*Mirror*: 65). While there may have been reason to snub the neglectful and even corrupt priests they encountered, Francis insisted that his friars respect and not alienate the local clergy (*Mirror*: 54). They were—as the most "minor" servants of God—to subject themselves to the will of the bishops and not seek special privileges from the pope:

> You Friars Minor don't understand God's will and won't allow me to convert the whole world the way God wills. For first of all I want to convert the bishops by our holy humility and respect. When they come to see our holy way of life and our humble respect for them, they will ask you to preach and convert the people. These things will draw people to your preaching far better than your privileges, which would only lead you into pride (*Mirror*: 50).

The regular clergy had every reason to ignore or even to censure a popular holy man like Francis. Since the year 800 at the very latest, nearly every village in Christendom had some religious hero whose memory it revered as a "saint" and around whom superstitious cults were apt to spring up. Jealously preserving the theological precision of its doctrine, the official church did its best to discourage such movements, but wherever possible confirmed the theologically compliant by "canonizing" their local saint. The holy man of Assisi cannot be understood outside of this context. His mystical experimentation— regardless of his reverence for the church—took him outside the clear boundaries of orthodoxy. The church has always been suspicious of saints who are too much inspired by the Holy Spirit. Orthodoxy defends itself by curbing the idiosyncratic tendencies of its mystics—particularly those who inspire local cults and enthusiastic movements.

By the beginning of the thirteenth century, the situation had become dangerous. The people of the towns, finding the feudal organization of the church unsympathetic and irrelevant to their interests, wanted a faith based on intense personal experience that gave them an emotional connection with Christ, his mother, and the other saints. Part of their hostility to the priesthood had to do with the hierarchy and impersonality of the feudal world. In this context, Francis's spirituality appeared as a dangerous breath of fresh air. His emotional devotion and attention to the changes in consciousness brought on by his experiments in mysticism might have led to his becoming a heretical leader of a rebellion against the church. In fact, however, his determination to preach within the limits of established episcopal power, always yielding to the wishes of the local bishops, showed the way toward an urban religiosity that would enlarge and enliven the church's influence (Cantor, 1994: 187, 387, 429). Francis's respect for the church had its limits, however. He was concerned that ecclesiastical preoccupation with theological correctness was a great impediment to the sort of spiritual and transformative experience that made his way of life possible. His cautious ambivalence is expressed in a letter he wrote to the future St. Anthony of Padua: "It pleases me that you teach sacred theology to the brothers, as long as—in the words of the Rule—you 'do not extinguish the Spirit of prayer and devotion' with study of this kind" (Armstrong & Brady, 1982: 79).

The "Rule" Francis speaks of in this letter is the official Rule of Life for the Franciscan Order, promulgated in 1223; and the difference between this written papal document and the one that was orally approved in 1209 frames the greatest crisis in Francis's life. In a mere fourteen years, the spirit with which he and his first disciples had lived on the Rivo Torto had not only been forgotten but nearly legislated out of existence, assimilated to the needs and fears of a church that was larger than Assisi, larger than Europe, and had in its twelve centuries survived much greater threats than Francis's sadhana of poverty. In Francis's eyes, the church had distorted his vision and come near to having forbidden his way of life. His response to this monumental disappointment is described by his early biographers in the mythological language of apotheosis: Francis undergoes an agony like that of Jesus in the Garden of Olives, is crucified with the stigmata, and passes into a well-nigh angelic existence for the last two years of his mortal life.

The Curse of Success

According to the early biographies, Francis occasionally entered ecstasy to reassure himself of God's intentions for his order; and every time he did so, he received images of success, throngs from every country crowding the roads in their enthusiasm to don the brown robe and knotted rope of Franciscan brotherhood. Although these visions of wide-spread popularity turned out to be accurate, they proved a mixed blessing at best. Like the desert fathers of the second century in Egypt, the Franciscans saw their holy project diluted by multitudes of well-meaning but poorly disciplined followers. The archbishop of Perugia, Jacques de Vitry was alarmed: "There is a great danger in thus accepting pell-mell the perfect and the imperfect" (Englebert, 1979: 197). Less than a decade after Innocent III's informal approval of the first twelve friars' way of life, the order had swelled into the thousands; and most of these new friars barely knew Francis, certainly had not learned the spirit of the Rivo Torto, and found themselves answering to superiors chosen for their learning and ecclesiastical prominence, men who represented the status quo in the church rather than the sadhana of poverty, clerics who considered Francis himself to be a "dangerous visionary" (*Ibid.*, 170). In short, the Franciscans were becoming as motley a throng as those Qalandars of central Asia with their small core of genuine mystics and many hangers-on "of slight mystical pretension."

There is a sense in some of the reports that all of this was happening behind Francis's back. For example, *The Legend of Perugia* (33) says, "As long as the holy Father lived, the brothers of this friary [the Portiuncula] sat on the ground to eat, thereby conforming to his example and will." Even if they did not bring in dining tables and chairs immediately after his death, the message is clear that it was hard to maintain the spirit of Francis's sadhana in the absence of the saint's "example and will." We have no reason to assume bad faith on the part of the friars. Rather the fact is that Francis's mentality and daily practice lay so far beyond the thinking of his contemporaries that they had little hope of maintaining it without his charismatic presence. Many stories illustrate this theme, including the tragic story of Brother Leo, who began a grandiose building program shortly after Francis's death.

While Francis was in Syria trying to convert Muslims, a rumor began that he was dead, and the friars back home were at a loss for what to do: "Some of Francis's closest friends took refuge in the hermitages; other Brothers wandered about at their own sweet will, and one of them collected a following of male and female lepers who wished to be included in the Fraternity" (de Robeck, 1980: 57). On his return from the Middle East, Francis found the friars of Bologna living in a fine house that they "regarded as their own property" (Frugoni, 1998: 107). Even the Portiuncula itself had been contaminated with "ownership," for he found that a large building of stone had been built adjacent to the chapel to accommodate the hundreds of friars that came regularly to attend "chapter meetings" to discuss the nature of their common life and adopt changes as they seemed necessary. Enraged at the existence of this new building and its flagrant contrast with the spirit of poverty, Francis climbed onto the roof and began ripping off tiles and throwing them to the ground. He would have single-handedly destroyed the building but eventually was convinced that it had been built by the citizens of Assisi, that it belonged to them and not to the friars, although the citizens allowed the friars to use it (*Perugia*: 11). Even with this explanation, the new building represented a major compromise with the spirit of the Rivo Torto. Everywhere Francis looked, it seemed, his order was losing its connection with the mystical experiments that gave it birth.

Such confusions over the nature of Francis's sadhana are basic to the history of the Franciscan Rule of Life. In fact, the order had three "Rules." The first, orally approved Rule of 1209 has been "lost." Presumably what happened is that Francis tinkered with it for years, adding scripture verses to illustrate and justify its provisions, and making adaptations as chapter meetings proposed them. By 1221, it had become the second Rule, the very lengthy "Unpromulgated Rule" (Regula non Bullata). When presented before the general chapter meeting of 1221, the second Rule threatened to split the order and aroused objections from the church as well. Over the next two years a new, much shorter, and far less original document was hammered out between the Cardinal-Protector of the order (the future Pope Gregory IX) and the Ministers General of the several Franciscan provinces. This third Rule eliminated nearly everything related to the sadhana of poverty, including the recommendation that friars should disobey any superior who would interfere with their literal observance of the gospels, the prescription that they should do nothing to prevent their residences or clothing being taken from them, and that they should own no books.

The Mirror of Perfection gives us Francis's response to this ecclesiastical corruption of his vision. According to the story, a number of "prudent and learned" friars asked the Cardinal-Protector to persuade Francis to accept "the wise guidance" of earlier monastic rules. Francis responded by taking the cardinal with him before the assembled friars, where he minced no words:

> And he spoke to the friars in the fervour and power of the Holy Spirit, saying, "My brothers! my brothers! God has called me by the way of simplicity and humility, and has in truth revealed this way for me and for all who are willing to trust and follow me. So I do not want you to quote any other Rule to me, whether it be that of Saint Benedict, Saint Augustine, or Saint Bernard, or to recommend any other way or form of life except this way which God in His mercy has revealed and given to me. The Lord told me that He wished me to be a new kind of simpleton in this world, and He does not wish us to live in any other wisdom but this. God will confound you through your own prudence and learning. And I trust in the constables of God [i.e., the devils], that He will punish you through them. Eventually, whether you wish it or not, you will return with great remorse to your first state."
>
> The Cardinal was utterly dumbfounded and said nothing; and all the friars were filled with great fear (*Mirror*: 68).

The Great Temptation
Clearly it was not only the bureaucratic church that had chastely put away Francis's holy concubine, Lady Poverty. His own friars had cooperated, and primarily because he had lost touch with them. Their

numbers were too great. Popular success had defeated mystic sub-stance. No doubt the numbers of friars attending chapter meetings between 1217 and 1221 have been greatly exaggerated by the early biographers, where five thousand men are weaving themselves tempo-rary shelters out of reeds and rushes for the week of the meeting. But even hundreds of disciples would have been too many for Francis to have influenced personally or carefully trained in the sadhana of poverty and ecstasy. Apostleship to the towns and a theologically sound emotional spirituality were enough for most of them. To this they added very reasonable assumptions from their medieval mindset: traditional monastic rules and asceticism together with a more intel-lectual effort at articulating their town-oriented spirituality.

Francis lived only three years beyond the promulgation of the third and final Rule, and by that time his followers had split into three factions (Habig, 1983: 1275). The "Moderates" tried to revise the sad-hana of poverty so that they could perform the more intellectual and clerical work the church was giving them. The "Relaxed" pretty much gave up all pretension of poverty and the pursuit of ecstasy, leaving them very little "Franciscan" apart from their dress. Finally, the "Spirituals" or "Zealots" were rigorous in their pursuit of ecstasy and fanatical followers of the mystical philosopher Joachim di Fiori (1135–1202) who had divided world history into three ages: the Age of the Father, which preceded the birth of Jesus; the Age of the Son, which occupied the first millennium of Christianity; and the Age of the Holy Spirit, which, he said, was just beginning. The Franciscan "Spirituals" believed they were hastening this "New Age"—along with hundreds of heretical and half-baked movements that perpetrated mayhem throughout Europe and the Middle East for centuries (Cohn, 1970). Not one of these Franciscan factions was trying to be a "new kind of simpleton in this world."

The chapter meeting of 1221, when Francis presented the Rule he had been lovingly perfecting for a dozen years, was riven by passion-ate debate as the precursors of the three factions encountered one another's vision of the Franciscan way of life. Francis was shocked and enraged: "Who are these who have snatched my order and that of my brothers out of my hands?" (*2Celano*: 188). He spoke of divine retri-bution and seemed confident that God would eventually provide it. His biographers describe the two years between the hubbub when

Francis first formally presented his Rule and the approval in 1223 of its politically correct revision as the time of Francis's "Great Temptation." They are resolutely opaque over what he was tempted to do. Nevertheless, we can be confident he never considered relinquishing the sadhana of poverty, and his respect for the church was too great for him to want to found a religion of his own and declare himself a heretic. There can only be one thing he was tempted to do—to abandon his order to its boring and pointless fate. Half-baked friars would become just another troop of volunteers carrying out the empty designs of a church that refused to attend to its consciousness. Let them go their conventional way. He would take whatever handful of faithful practitioners of poverty that remained. Be they three, as in the days of Bernard and Sylvester, or twelve as when they walked to Rome with their first Rule, they would live the life of trading downward and keep themselves in God's Vast Earth with occasional bouts of dharma preaching. They would not be "Franciscans." They would be God's simpletons. And if anyone thought they were heretics or highwaymen, they would thank God for their share in the sufferings of Christ.

The great two-year-long temptation is variously presented by the biographers. Bonaventure takes up an account of Celano and gives it a somewhat more "saintly" twist. He says that Francis sought out deserted places to pray, believing that the more remote the location and the fewer the distractions the more likely the Holy Spirit would conduct him into ecstasy. What he faced there, though, as a sort of first stage in changing his consciousness, was an "assault" by devils. Francis is said to be engaged in "hand-to-hand combat" with them; and although the struggles were "horrible," Francis came through victorious and ended by speaking with his divine lover. In "proof" of this conclusion, Francis is said to have been seen "raised up from the ground" in a "miraculous light" as he prayed with his arms extended as though in identification with the crucified Christ (*2Celano*: 119–23; *MajLife*: X, 3; *MinLife*: IV, 2).

These accounts imply a variation on Francis's earlier experiments in narcissism. In those younger, happier days, Francis exposed himself deliberately and resolutely to his own sinful past, the shadow of his former and habitual failings. He entered thoroughly into his shame while standing before the Lord of the whole earth. There was no mention of devils or of hand-to-hand combat. It was clear that Francis himself was the enemy, especially the Francis of past shameful deeds. Now, however, during the Great Temptation, it is a future deed that generates his shame, a deed he does not wish to confess and put behind him. His rage, his feelings of abandonment, and his glorious memories of dalliance in ecstasy with his lover: all these things drive him toward abandoning his order. It would be an act of scorn for the temporizers, the tepid, the self-important, and the resolutely ignorant. It would be a passionate act of love, a flagrant elopement with Lady Poverty.

Formerly Francis could say to himself, "Yes, I have failed, and I stand before God confessing my failure; but God forgives me and draws me into the ecstatic world." He knew that he did not deserve to be forgiven and that he would be drawing upon these same failings next time he courted narcissism. Now, however, forgiveness is out of the question, for the deed has not been committed. Furthermore, he is not sorry for contemplating it. He revels in the idea of it, as radical an act as stripping before the bishop. He stands before God—not in his shame, this time—but in his willfulness. Is this a lovers' quarrel? Has God become as much his enemy as his beloved?

The Devils

Before Thomas of Celano and Bonaventure wrote of devils physically assaulting the saint, Brother Leo had described the struggle in rather more psychological language.

> Francis . . . wanted to rest and sleep. But he could not, for his mind was beset with fear and disturbed by suggestions from the Devil. He got up immediately, went outside of the church and made the sign of the cross, saying: "Devils! I command you on behalf of God almighty to make my body suffer. I am ready to endure everything, for I have no greater enemy than my body; in this way you will avenge me on this adversary and enemy." The suggestions ceased immediately. Returning to the place where he wanted to spend the night, he fell asleep and rested peacefully (*Perugia*: 23).

If Leo was truly the author of this "legend," we can think that, as Francis's scribe, nurse, and confessor, he is giving us an inside perspective on his mentor's struggle. The devils did not come to pummel but to scare him to death and make suggestions that were nearly beyond his power to resist. They had no designs on "Brother Ass" but were after Francis's soul, trying to entice him into a self-damning decision, a betrayal of everything his saintly life seemed to stand for. Furthermore, Francis must have been genuinely uncertain about which decision to take: to be faithful to the sadhana of poverty or to the hierarchical church. To go one way was to embrace heresy and perhaps lead thousands into enmity with the church and with God— the course Joachim di Fiori had taken a couple of generations earlier, very likely in all sincerity though the damage to the church and civil society was unmistakable[54] To go the other way was to repudiate all that his experiments had taught him about cultivating ecstasy and divine intimacy, to declare his life's work a failure, and to cooperate in the humiliation of Lady Poverty.

A century later, *The Mirror of Perfection* remembers that Francis suffered "a violent beating" by devils when he lay himself down to sleep one night. This time there is no reference to the Great Temptation; rather Francis is in Rome meeting with "the Lord Pope and Cardinals," who "venerated him as a saint" and offered him a room in a secluded tower "where [he] could live as though in a hermitage." Francis graciously accepts, and the devils take him by surprise. He is awake the whole night with his companion, shaking as though in a fever. At some point before dawn, however, he figures out the meaning of the attack:

> The devils are God's constables, for just as the authorities send a constable to punish a wrong-doer, so does God correct and punish those whom He loves through the devils who are His constables and act as His servants in this office. Even a perfect Religious often sins in ignorance; consequently, if he does not realize his sin, he is punished by the devil so that he may realize and carefully consider how he may have sinned, whether inwardly or outwardly (*Mirror*: 67).

Francis goes on to say that he is unaware of an unconfessed and unatoned sin that might be responsible for this attack by the devils, but has concluded that his "lodging with a cardinal" may set a bad example for friars "who live in squalid little huts." He therefore leaves the tower early in the morning and returns "to the hermitage of Fonte Colombo, near Riete."

Although the author of *Mirror* seems blissfully unaware of ecclesiastical politics, very likely he is not; for this anecdote zeroes in on the issue that lies behind the Great Temptation—the conflict between the "sainthood" church authorities want to "venerate" in Francis and the sadhana of poverty that brought him to this point. The story implies that Francis remained blissfully unaware of the conflict until he lay down to sleep. His meetings with pope and cardinals had apparently aroused no conscious suspicions—very much as he had seemed to present his Rule to the chapter meeting of 1221 without foreseeing the opposition it would arouse. Perhaps there is a narcissistic element in his blindness to the conflict, something subtle in the flattery he received from the most powerful individuals in the church that lulls him into acquiescence. They would place him in a remote tower on the pretext that nothing will interfere with his prayer, not mentioning that this lofty honor will elevate him beyond having influence over his order and their church. He accepts naïvely, but interference enters the picture as soon as his conscious tension slackens. Devils emerge from his unconscious. His "pre-conscious" grasp of the political implications of praying in a remote tower begins to register. Although still too vaguely defined to be conceptualized, he feels the conflict as an assault by a horde of beings more powerful than he.

Devils are common in the religious literature of the European Middle Ages and still a staple of Christian discourse, especially among the most conservative and literal-minded. But the early Franciscan biographers write extremely sparingly of them. Devils attack Francis only when his mind is occupied with the most serious matters, when he is trying to reconcile his love for the church with his courtship of Lady Poverty. They make no appearance when he has been thoughtless of or disrespectful to another friar; they never try to distract him from his prayer or tempt him into making luxurious provisions for himself. His outbursts of anger, too, are generally inspired by lofty intentions. His devils, therefore, have little in common with such caricatures as the Ayatollah Khomeini's "Great Satan," the Antichrist of Christian lore, or the naughty schemer who "made me do it." They are not so much tempters as tormentors, not God's adversaries but God's constables. Dark and unpleasant though they may be, they are as much God's emissaries as are the bright angels. Indeed, they are the faces of God, the effects of God's actions as we experience them. We encounter them only when they act upon us. We feel only their effects. Just as the God we experience impinges upon our unconscious faculties so as to generate visions, intuitions, and feelings, so the angels as "God's messengers" and the devils as "God's constables" are distinguishable from God perhaps only insofar as their effects are less numinous.

The devils in these accounts, therefore, are subjective factors of a peculiarly "impersonal" sort. They are subjective in the sense that Francis experiences them: he is filled with fear, impressed with his own impotence, shivers uncontrollably, and needs the presence and support of his companion. At the same time, the devils are "impersonal" in the sense that their power seems to come from elsewhere. They are completely ego-alien, frighteningly uncanny, and wholly unpredictable. In the *Mirror* anecdote, we are informed that Francis was consciously at ease with himself and untroubled by guilt when God's constables arrived. Celano and Bonaventure give us a more shaken Francis, one uncertain of what to do but still not at all in conflict with his conscience. Apparently it is simply because Francis sees no conflict that the devils approach with their disturbing suggestions. Horrifying and unprecedented thoughts emerge that are too grotesque even for Francis, "the most ungrateful of God's creatures." But in the most fundamental sense they are God's thoughts, for they come at God's bidding, brought by God's constables.

In short, the devils represent the dark side of ecstasy. We should not be surprised to learn that ecstasy has its disturbing, even threatening side. The classic nineteenth century phenomenology of ecstatic experience, Rudolf Otto's *The Idea of the Holy* (1917/58) defines "the Holy" as the *mysterium tremendum et fascinans*, the mystery that makes us tremble and fascinates us. When Moses asks Yahweh to show him the "glory" that would confirm the Lord's godhood, he is told, "No man may look upon me and live" (Exodus 33:22). Similarly, the divinities of India and Tibet all have two aspects, often distinguished as "blissful" and "wrathful." Kali, the Black One, for example, is always shown with a necklace of human skulls and a skirt of human arms, wielding a sword. Sometimes she is dancing on the dead body of her consort. Despite her "wrathful" aspect, however, she is one of the most loved divinities in India, revered as "the Mother" who destroys ignorance and brings her devotees to liberation.

The End of Simplicity

Given this universal human history wherein the ecstatic realm comprises both that which fulfills us beyond all expectation and horrifies us with immanent destruction, we have to think there is a reason why the biographies of Francis reserve all mention of "God's constables" to the rather later period when the sadhana of poverty seems to have come in conflict with the authorities of the church and divided even the friars into factions. It seems that Francis's vaunted simplicity has been seriously challenged. Until now it has been enough for him to know a God only of bliss and joy. But the crisis that has been brewing in the shadows behind his back has changed things for good. The "perfect joy" that could not be dimmed by icicles banging against his ankles or rejection by the porter of his hermitage seemed to prove that he had transcended internal conflict, for no discomfort could touch his joy or lessen it. But now division within the order has shocked him and stirred up a rage that reveals an unconscious division within himself: poverty or obedience, acquiescence in tepidity or righteous rebellion.

Looked at psychologically, the blissful gods differ from their wrathful counterparts not in who they are but in how we are affected by them. The disparity in their aspect reflects our dividedness. The wrathful, "constabulary" God horrifies and frightens us by opposing attitudes we have taken for granted and assumed were devoted, spiritual, and praiseworthy. God's constables go after our narrowness and rigidity, pummel us for our blindness, attempt to open us up to a wider, more inclusive perspective, liberate us from our ego-centered notions, and destroy our ignorance. The more we hang onto what we have been, the more excruciating the wrathful encounter and the more we need God's constables. We can only conclude, therefore, that the "sainthood" so roundly praised in the simple Poverello who brought his amended and polished Rule before the chapter meeting of 1221 had to be challenged by a painful encounter on both planes of reality. While ecclesiastical politics banished his beloved Lady Poverty in negotiations by day, God's constables were torturing him by night.

In short, the devils compensated for the unconsciousness of Francis's straightforward simplicity. Perhaps it would have been enough merely to practice the sadhana of poverty, had Francis attracted only a dozen or so disciples, all of whom could learn the experimental methods directly from him and be guided by his example; for that approach was clearly working at the time they went to Rome for papal approval. Ten years later it had become too naïve. Now there were hundreds—possibly thousands—of "Franciscan" styles of life to challenge the one Francis and his earliest followers had discovered on the banks of the Rivo Torto. "Franciscanism" was becoming amorphous, and the official church was stepping in to give it a traditional form. It was only natural for the church to think in terms of established monasticism and the hierarchy of clerics, the very things that denied the uniqueness and validity of Francis's experimentation and discovery.

When the cosmic joy of pouring-through was simple, Francis took delight participating in the passing down of a fur cloak from a wealthy woman of style to a bedraggled beggar. He warned his benefactor to get ready for the shock, and believed that dealing with that narcissistic blow was an important part of her spiritual practice. Like a refiner's fire, the sadhana of poverty burns dross from the souls of its practitioners. With the disappearance of simplicity, however, it was not only things, inanimate objects, that pour through and become altered beyond recognition by their participation in the cosmic process. Now ecclesiastical negotiations were subjecting the ecstatic technique of poverty itself to the distortions of being passed down from conscious practitioners to the ignorant and unprepared. On the Rivo Torto, poverty had been a divinely inspired sadhana, a humble but reliable road to God. Now it was in danger of becoming an affectation, a badge, a way of signaling a certain style or political affiliation within the church. Radical experimentation in revision and renewal was being co-opted by the complacent behemoth it was meant to reform.

The practice of poverty had taught Francis a thoroughgoing detachment from things. Although he had been inclined in that direction already as a partying youth, giving everything away for the sake of a good time, his holy experiments expanded upon that base and taught him to relinquish pleasure, fame, and social status. The constabulary God, however, laid a hand on the one item from which Francis seemed unable to detach, his ascetic practice—for how could he be indifferent to poverty without being indifferent to God? Poverty was the method he had discovered for setting his ego aside in favor of a greater will, his participation in the cosmic process of pouring-through. Poverty was the source of his intimacy with God; and now God, as it seemed, through the hierarchy of the church, was requiring that real poverty, gospel poverty, a poverty based in remaining conscious of one's psychic states was being rejected as inessential at best and dangerous at worst.

The discipline of poverty was what God had given Francis through the inspiration of the Holy Spirit. It was his living connection with God, and he saw it as the foundation of a humble movement that would reform the church from within. He could not conceive that it was not God's will that this simple and humble path be made available for all to follow. Yet, here it was: God was destroying what God had wrought. This was a darker God that Francis had bargained for, a relative of the God who had ordered the prophet Hosea to marry a prostitute and Abraham to sacrifice his son. No wonder Francis offered those devils his body to torture: the simple foe, the "adversary and enemy" against which the sadhana of poverty had already proven so effective.

Bodily suffering was fully compatible with "perfect joy" and could not interfere with his rest. Francis, therefore, seems to have outsmarted God in getting the devils out of his mind and into his body. No doubt he succeeded in this ploy by attending to his consciousness. If the devils could so thoroughly occupy his mind that they made him forget the pain of the trachoma in his eyes, then he would simply have to attend to his pain and let that drown out the doubts and suggestions of impossible complexity that had been assailing his mind. It was altogether too slick, a regressive move, a retreat from the challenge to his simplicity that God had ordained. But he got what he wanted. He lapsed into restful sleep.

Acceptance

The Great Temptation continued, however, until Francis could bring himself to let go of his personal mystic path, accepting that it would likely be lost forever. Simultaneously, he let go of the order and allowed it become what the hierarchical church wanted it to be. Realistically, he had no choice. But apparently ignorant of that fact, he wrestled to the end. According to the outward story, Francis's longtime friend Hugolini de Segni,[55] the Cardinal-Protector of the Franciscan Order and most powerful member of the Roman Curia, the church's governing body, persuaded Francis that the church needed the quasi-monastic teaching order that he and the provincial ministers had described in their final version of the Franciscan Rule. God had spoken through the authorities of the church, and Francis as a good Catholic and a saint could hardly refuse to relinquish the sadhana of poverty as the order's governing principle.

The inner story of Francis's acquiescence is told in three of the early biographies, in nearly the same words every time (*2Celano*: 115; *Mirror*: 99; *Perugia*: 21). It is 1223, just about two years before his death, and Francis has been wrestling with his conscience day and night since the chapter meeting in 1221 when his preferred version of the Rule had caused such opposition. He is at the Portiuncula, fasting, avoiding contact with the friars, and drowning in the agonies of the Great Temptation, when:

> . . . in spirit he heard this word of the gospel: "If your faith were the size of a mustard seed you could say to this mountain, 'Move from here to there,' and it would move." Blessed Francis asked: "What is this mountain?" "The mountain is your temptation." "Then, Lord, may it be done to me according to your word." And immediately he was freed of it, so much so that it seemed to him that he had never been troubled by that temptation" (*Perugia*: 21).

The author of *Perugia*, perhaps Brother Leo, tells within the space of two pages both this story and the one about how Francis commanded the devils to attack his body. Presented with separate traditions on how Francis came to terms with the crisis in the order, Leo tells us both as though they are equivalent.[56] A moment's reflection will reveal, however, that they differ in every respect. The enraged Poverello shouting commands at the devils is in something of a narcissistic funk, saying in effect: How dare you mess with my mind and conscience? Don't you know I have discovered the sadhana of poverty and become intimate with God? Go back to the petty temptations of the flesh where you belong. Increase my physical pain, but let me rest in my simplicity. This is Francis's ego in high dudgeon demanding he not be disturbed in the spiritual life-course he has been refining for perhaps two decades. True enough, he worked out the crisis in dialogue with God and his own unconscious, but by the time of the Great Temptation it has become a *conscious* achievement he refuses for very good reason to relinquish.

The story about the mountain moving, however, is quite different. This time the agency comes from elsewhere; and although its source is unidentified at the start, it becomes clear before long that Francis takes it to be the voice of God. An ego-alien, autonomous movement emerges from his unconscious at a moment when Francis has thinned out his ego-membrane by fasting and isolation and speaks the words of Christ in the Gospel of Matthew (17:20). Jesus' disciples—not unlike Francis—have been trying unsuccessfully to cast out devils and go to their master in private to find out what they have been doing wrong. Jesus says they have no faith at all, whereas they would be successful if they had the tiniest smidgen of it—a speck the size of a mustard seed.

Mustard seed occurs in only two contexts in the New Testament: the present story about moving the mountain (also Luke 17: 6) and the parable describing the kingdom of heaven as "like a mustard seed," which is the smallest of seeds but grows into a huge bush (Matthew 13:31; Mark 4:31; Luke 13:19). Francis, his friars, and his biographers were steeped in the words and images of the Bible. No reference passed their notice; even their dreams were dense with scriptural imagery. The mustard-seed image, for them, was highly specific. Faith and the kingdom of heaven are, at bottom, the same thing: that perspective wherein the ecstatic world surrounds, interpenetrates, and reveals the ultimate meaning of every event that occurs in the empirical world. The smallest degree (a "mustard seed") of openness to a world of meaning transcending the conventional makes everything possible: the moving of mountains, the casting out of devils, and the ecstasy by which God draws near and reveals even this world to belong to the Vast Earth of Reality.

The autonomous, ego-alien voice, therefore, directs Francis's attention to something he has long been familiar with, the results of his sadhana. The spiritual practice of poverty had unveiled his own mustard seed, which had grown into "the greatest of shrubs . . . so that the birds of the air [had] come and [made] nests in its branches" (Matthew 13:31). Francis could hardly consider it just another possession to hand over to the cosmic pouring-through. It was not something he possessed but a technique he had discovered for passing out of the profane world and into the sacred cosmos. Above all, he wanted to pass on to his friars and the world at large this simple precondition of ecstasy, the thing that made mustard seeds possible. But the voice he heard in the midst of his Great Temptation said clearly enough: This, too, must go. Forget what you thought was your unique and irreplaceable contribution. Have faith that God knows better than you do.

The insight that voice brought to Francis is almost identical to the central teaching of the *Bhagavad Gita* (Deutsch, 1968):

> In action only has thou a right and never in its fruits. Let not thy motive be the fruits of action; nor let thy attachment be to inaction.
>
> Fixed in yoga, O winner of wealth, perform actions, abandoning attachment and remaining even-minded in success and failure; for serenity of mind is called yoga (II: 47–8).

"Serenity of mind" has been the issue all along for Francis. In the early experiments, narcissism was his guide, the problem of how to stand up to the disturbing force of those emotions—how to court the radical upset of a narcissistic crisis while maintaining his equilibrium. Standing down the demons of narcissism has been the heart of his sadhana. But at this late moment in his mystical life, Francis finds himself unable to "remain even-minded in success and failure." He is attached to his daily practice, and not just for himself; he knows its potential for transforming the church and the world, and feels he has an obligation to defend it. He still has a powerful impulse to preach the truth of what he has learned: the example of life on the Rivo Torto, the ultimate pointer toward perfect joy. He is not simply practicing his poverty, but has a powerful interest in its "fruits." He cares how things work out.

The voice tells him, in effect, to move that mountain of concern over the fruitfulness of his actions. He can do so by handing them over to God, by having "faith" that all will be worked out in some unspecified future planned by a divine intention that exceeds his own understanding. When he paraphrases the Lord's Prayer, "May it be done to me according to your word," he wholly alters his stance. He drops all interest in how things will work out, "so that it seemed to him that he had never been troubled by that temptation." In the language of the *Bhavagad Gita*, Francis's "action" is the practice of poverty. Once his mountain has been moved, he returns to that sadhana without concern for results and with no temptation to flee into "inaction." On being urged, later, to intervene in the government of the order, Francis is unshakable, "The friars already know what to do and what to avoid, so that no duty remains for me except to set them an example by my own actions" (*Mirror*: 81).

Transcendence

Francis's last gesture toward reminding his friars of his life of experimental poverty, courting narcissism, and living in the cosmos of ecstasy, was to write his "Testament" as a sort of addendum to the churchly Rule that had been approved. He chose not to fight to make it an official part of that Rule but believed it would always accompany the Rule. Nevertheless, his friend and protector, Gregory IX, severed its connection with the Rule two years after the Poverello's death. Larger-than-life forces seemed determined to cut Francis, the individual, loose from the movement he had started.

Although he wrote a "Testament" upon emerging from the Great Temptation, he never looked back. He became, in the vision of his hagiographers, an ephemeral, superhuman being, a sort of minor divinity. They outdo one another in presenting a man who had somehow slipped the bounds of his flesh. He underwent what would cause the rest of us prodigious pain (the cauterization of his temples) without undue discomfort. People snipped swatches of putative relics from his clothing as he passed through their midst, insensate with ecstasy. His feet no longer touched the ground, as his infirmities—including the stigmata—made walking impossible. His face was hooded against the slightest gleam of light for the pain it would cause. The collective ecstasy of Christmas at Greccio in 1223, with its chain of miracles, was the only luminous moment during the period of the temptation, but it set the tone for the stories that followed Francis's ultimate detachment (Frugoni, 1998: 113).

There is a third and final account of how the Great Temptation ended, not necessarily incompatible with the stories of commanding the devils and moving the mountain. But if those other stories prompt us to speak of "resolution" or "detachment," this ultimate tale suggests "apotheosis," for it ends with the stigmata. In the summer of 1224, Francis set out for the mountain retreat of LaVerna, a hundred miles north of Assisi, in what seems to have been a deliberate attempt to recreate the spirit of the Rivo Torto. He took five companions—Leo, Angelo, Illuminato, Rufino, and Masseo—and traveled without itinerary, sleeping wherever the temporary superior, Masseo, deemed appropriate. They ate begged bread; and as they walked, they recited the prayers appointed for the hours, practiced dharma preaching, or kept silent (Englebert, 1979: 236). They spent whole nights in contemplation and, like Moses in the desert, Francis caused water to flow from a rock when they were thirsty (*Flowers*, Part II: pp. 1434–5; *2Celano*: 46). After they had arrived at LaVerna to a welcome from the birds, Francis imitated Christ on the Mount of Olives, leaving his disciples behind so as to wrestle with his demons in isolation. He began a "lent" in honor of St. Michael the Archangel, six weeks of prayer and fasting modeled after the familiar lent that precedes Easter.

The "Michaelmas Lent" was a well-known devotion in Francis's day and very much "angelic" in its theme. It began on the feast of the Assumption of the Blessed Virgin, August 15, which commemorates the "angelification" of the mother of Jesus, in that she is said to have been "assumed body and soul into heaven,"[57] and ended on the feast of the Archangel Michael, September 29. As with the lent of late winter, it involved fasting and the denial of the body's needs—a dramatic exercise that seeks to "angelify" the human practitioner by bringing the body into line and making it serve the spirit. For Francis—who called St. Mary of the Angels home—this late summer lent meant a retreat from preaching, where one had to make concessions to the conventional world in order to convince one's hearers. He could immerse himself completely in the "angelic" activity of contemplation. He accepted supplies from his companions, but only upon a pre-determined signal, lest they barge in and disturb his ecstasy. Characteristically, Leo was too curious to observe the letter of the rule and is said to have witnessed Francis levitating more than once (*Flowers*: Part II, pp. 1444–5).

The forty days of Francis's lent corresponded to the forty years the Israelites wandered in the wilderness, the forty days and nights of rain that purified the world of sinners in the days of Noah, and the forty days Jesus fasted and prayed before beginning his public ministry. These mythic correspondences were not lost on Francis. He immersed himself in the Bible every day, reciting favorite verses as a Hindu does his mantra, following hour by hour the suffering and death of Jesus' last day in the "Office of the Passion" he composed. If the biographers do not overlard too much in their piety, we have to think that Francis saw biblical parallels everywhere: in the worms he carefully saved from the roadway, and scraps of scribbled paper whose words could be reassembled to spell out divine names or verses from scripture. Thus, he could hardly have been wholly unconscious of identifying with Christ when he took a handful of his closest disciples to a mountain top and then went a bit apart from them to enter an agonized ecstasy.

Francis had been fasting and praying thirty days when the church celebrated the Exultation of the Holy Cross in its liturgy, and his own identification with Christ became "somatized" in the wounds of the stigmata. On September 14, 1224, while rapt in contemplation, Francis had a vision of a crucified angel—a fiery, six-winged seraph, reminiscent of the one that appeared to the prophet Isaiah, except that it was nailed to a cross as Jesus had been. Shortly thereafter, Francis discovered the wounds of the nails in his own hands and feet. This is the essence of the earliest account, which also adds that the vision filled Francis with joy and fear:

> When the blessed servant of the Most High saw these things,
> he was filled with the greatest wonder, but he could not

understand what this vision should mean. Still, he was filled
with happiness and he rejoiced very greatly because of the
kind and gracious look with which he saw himself regarded by
the seraph, whose beauty was beyond estimation; but the fact
that the seraph was fixed to a cross and the sharpness of his
suffering filled Francis with fear. And so he arose, if I may so
speak, sorrowful and joyful, and joy and grief were in him
alternately. Solicitously he thought what this vision could
mean, and his soul was in great anxiety to find its meaning
(*1Celano*: 94).

Later accounts add incidental details of greater or lesser probabil-
ity: that the seraph had the face of Jesus Christ, that shepherds saw
what seemed to be a forest fire, or that Leo regularly passed into ecstasy while changing the bandages on Francis's wounds.

According to the mind of the Middle Ages, an omnipotent agent
wholly other than Francis's puny ego sent him a bodiless being of
wondrous glory as a sort of message. Faced with the problem of deci-
phering the vision, Francis recalled three pairs of wings and a fiery
nature, facts that led him to Isaiah. When Bonaventure adds that the
appearance of the seraph caused Francis to burn with love in a sort of
shaktipat effect (Habig, 1983: 842), he may be referring to the theology of Bernard of Clairvaux, who a century earlier had said that the
seraphim are enflamed with divine love because they are "one spirit
with God" (Schmucki, 1991: 203). It makes more sense for us mod-
erns, however, to think that the vision *began* in Francis's psychic state
of inflammation by love, rage, and pain—that these overwhelming
emotions were the source of the vision. Francis's emotional state
expressed the nature of his problematic relationship with God, and the
vision clarified this experience—gave it some shape and made it loose-
ly comprehensible. Thus God sent Francis not a messenger but an
experience of flaming unity. The angel is a sort of third participant in
the love affair between God and Francis—the link, the point where
human emotion and divine essence are joined.

We can accept much of the medieval take on these events—even
if we carefully word things so as to keep God's role obscure. Francis's
unconscious—which has abundant biblical imagery at its disposal—

produces the best image it can come up with to mirror his emotional state of mind. He is, indeed, burning with love; but also with rage; and pierced by betrayal and abandonment. He feels at one with Christ's last words, "My God, my God, why hast Thou forsaken me?" LaVerna is his Sinai, his Mount of Olives, his Calvary, his Tabor. He is meeting God for the first time, agonizing over his temptation, crucifying his ego, shining in ecstasy. The God who manifests in this seraph is both wrathful and blissful, the unifier of the opposites, the mysterium tremendum et fascinans, the confluence of joy, grief, fear, and awe. Both God and Francis have become more complex.

Stigmata

The stigmata surely glorified Francis, for the pattern of five wounds was seen by his contemporaries and the generations that followed to be the ultimate confirmation of his sainthood by a miraculous divine intervention. It seemed as though God had made a point of distinguishing the Poverello and his way of life with an undeniable, physical sign. Francis may even have seen it that way himself, for he took special care to conceal the evidence of the wounds as he had long done to disguise the symptoms of his ecstasies. He acted almost as though the wounds were a matter of shame, hiding them so well that it was a long time before even his closest friends became aware of them. Even after they became a matter of common knowledge among the companions, "he nevertheless took it ill if anyone looked at them" (*2Celano*: 135–6). They constituted a narcissistic challenge in that Francis was vulnerable to falling into feelings of grandiosity and vainglory; and if he should ever succumb to self-congratulation or pride, he would be sure to be plunged immediately into the misery of shame at having arrogated to his ego what had simply been a gift from God.

The old narcissistic issues he had used for so many years to guide his simple practice of poverty continued and were, in fact, exacerbated by the stigmata. But there was evidently a darker and more disturbing fact to deal with, for *The Mirror of Perfection* says, "When he received the Stigmata of our Lord in his own body on the holy mountain of LaVerna, he suffered so many temptations and troubles from the devils that he could not display his former joy," a fact he is said to have confessed to Brother Leo (*Mirror*: 99). Apparently the devils had not been outsmarted or vanquished; and if the mountain of his temptation had been moved, its new location did not bring him much relief from the torments that accompanied it.

The reasonably healthy man who walked a hundred miles with five companions, sleeping under the stars, eating only what they could beg, climbing LaVerna under his own power, sleeping and fasting under a canopy of branches for some five weeks, helped only by an occasional delivery of supplies, has undergone a dreadful transformation. For now his mobility and everyday functioning are seriously impaired, and not only in a physical sense. After wrestling with the devils for two years, outsmarting them occasionally so as to sneak in a little rest, trying to neutralize them by putting all his faith in God, he has now come to realize he will never be free of them. They are an inseparable part of God. He may have relinquished his aspirations for the Franciscan Order, but he did so by putting his trust in a God as much wrathful as blissful—the God who had demanded the sacrifices of Isaac and Jesus. The painful and debilitating stigmata constituted the signature on a new mystical contract. The mountain was truly moved. It no longer stood before Francis but within.

It seems highly unlikely that the followers of Francis perpetrated a pious hoax in their reports of the stigmata. Prominent, critical-minded men were involved, and no alternate faction arose to deny it. Furthermore, although Francis was apparently the first stigmatic, the syndrome has appeared in hundreds of individuals in the eight centuries that have elapsed between his time and our own. The vast majority of these have been Roman Catholic, implying a socio-religious conditioning[58] More significantly, studies of recent stigmatics show that Francis had much in common with them: a medical history involving a variety of serious illnesses, a capacity for "somatizing" emotional conflicts as bodily symptoms, and an unusual propensity for ecstasies, visions, and other phenomena associated with a thinned-out ego-membrane (cf. Schmucki, 1991: 105). All these factors suggest Francis's body-and-mind were predisposed to a psychosomatic manifestation of mythic import.

To this picture, the biographers add a number of psychological details that show Francis had been preparing himself unconsciously for an identification with the crucified Christ. His mystical career began when the wooden figure of the crucified spoke to him; he had been meditating on the gospel accounts of Christ's passion every day for perhaps two decades; his favorite prayer was to beg God that he might feel the sufferings of Jesus in his own person; he was making a mystical retreat conditioned by two years of struggle with his Great Temptation; he thought of it as a "lent" that commemorated Jesus' forty-day retreat in the desert when he faced Satan's three great temptations; his daily practice on that retreat featured increased fasting and extended ecstasies that would surely have thinned out the boundary between conscious and unconscious regions of his psyche; and the vision that marked the appearance of the stigmata occurred on the feast of the Exultation of the Holy Cross, when the morning's liturgy included Paul's description of Christ as having emptied himself, poured out his divinity, "and accepted an obedience which brought him to death, death on a cross" (Philippians 2:5–11; The Roman Missal).

The angel theme is also highly significant: a man with a special devotion to angels makes a "lent" dedicated to an angel, calls contemplation an "angelic" activity, frequently designates his body, Brother Ass, as the enemy of his spiritual (therefore angelic) aspirations. Many of his ascetic efforts involve the suppression of his bodily needs and subsequent weakening of his constitution: preferring poor and unsanitary conditions for sleeping and eating, paying no attention to a balanced diet, serving and sharing the conditions of sick people, including lepers. In this context, it seems particularly significant that the overwhelming vision marking the climax of his story should be that of a crucified angel: a being bodiless by definition yet subjected to physical torment.

According to Francis's conscious mentality, it is his soul alone that counts for anything; his body is primarily an obstacle, at best an occasional instrument for other-worldly purposes. Since stripping before the bishop, he has often expressed a longing for martyrdom, the ultimate triumph of soul over body. There is a medieval simplicity to this mindset—all for the spiritual life of the soul, beginning with the mortification of the body. It worked very well for Francis, at least until the crisis at the chapter meeting in 1221. After that, in his Great Temptation, he has run up against something unprecedented that for two years has shown no sign of resolution. He is pulled in two directions at once: the sadhana of poverty or churchly business as usual, the self-evident proof of personal mystical experience against theological reasoning and clerical administration. Could both be the will of God? Can God be divided against God? Just then the image of a crucified seraph emerges from his unconscious, implying that it is the *spiritual* being that must be mortified. Even one enflamed with divine love because inseparable from the divine spirit, even one who poured out his divinity has been obedient unto crucifixion. Why not then Francis's soul?

That Francis bled from hands, feet, and side for the two years and a few days that remained to him suggests an hysterical "conversion," in Freud's language. Something "known" to be true in the unconscious expresses itself in a physical symptom. As a mechanism in hysteria, "conversion" implies a neurotic determination by the ego not to know something that is true of one's deeper being. I might, for instance, prefer to be paralyzed than know my incestuous wishes. If such neurotic subterfuge were true of Francis, we would have to think that he persisted in the simple formula that made his soul the source of all that is joyous and holy and his body the source of all that is profane and unworthy. This would be true of a man who could not allow his soul to be entered by the seraph that links him with God. The biographers do not describe such unconsciousness in Francis, rather the sight of the seraph churns up powerful and conflicting primal emotions in him. Francis seems to feel what the seraph feels while experiencing himself as the object of the angel's tender regard. His response is immediate and empathic. But he has no intellectual understanding:

> Solicitously he thought what this vision could mean, and his soul was in great anxiety to find its meaning. And while he was thus unable to come to any understanding of it and the strangeness of the vision perplexed his heart, the marks of the nails began to appear in his hands and feet, just as he had seen them a little before in the crucified man above him (*1Celano*: 94).

Here Francis does precisely what the hysteric cannot do. He reads the meaning of his vision in the symptoms of his body. Hysterics famously exhibit a *belle indifférence* toward their paralyses, blindnesses, and the like. Although the symptoms amount to the body-and-mind's last resort for bringing something to consciousness, the hysteric is unconsciously determined not to see what they mean. Francis, by contrast, is eager and anxious to know. When he sees the marks—Thomas of Celano wants us to believe—he connects them immediately with the seraph, with his love of God, and with the torment he has been undergoing. The "Passion" of Christ, Francis now sees, describes the same sort of rending love affair he himself has been pursuing. He, Christ, and the seraph are all in the same transcendent, anguished ecstasy. The last drop of divine essence that poured out of Christ on the cross courses through the seraph and cascades into Francis's transfixed soul, whence it runs away into the wounds of his flesh. The pouring-through has been realized in his own person in a heretofore unimaginable form, and with a torment he would have thought only two years before to be an impossibility. The opposites have been united in an awful and terrible way: bliss and torment, favor and punishment, soul and body, God and man.

Apotheosis

For the biographers, the stigmata was the crowning jewel in Francis's saintly life, the final proof that he was truly a second Christ, who not only lived as humbly, poorly, and purely as Jesus, but in whom an unprecedented miracle had proven beyond doubt that heaven and earth agree in their estimation of his holiness. His wounds form the linchpin in the argument and allow us to believe all those reports that involve Christ-like miracles. A brief sampling shows that they are closely patterned after gospel accounts of Jesus' miracles: multiplying food for a large audience (*1Celano*: 55), changing water into wine, stepping into a boat to avoid a crowd and having the boat move by divine command (*MinLife*: V, 9), healing a blind girl by applying his own spittle to her eyes three times in the name of the Trinity (*3Celano*: 124). In addition to these stories, there are reports of visions enjoyed by disciples that seem to show, when taken literally, that God has made it clear how favored and Christ-like in all respects Francis was. For example, Brother Peter of Montecchio is granted a vision of Christ crucified. Standing before the cross are John the beloved disciple, Mary the mother of Jesus, and Francis with his stigmata. As Peter contemplates this vision, he wonders which of these three lovers of Christ has suffered the most grievously over Jesus' crucifixion, whereupon all three appear to Peter, "and our blessed Father Francis, dressed in very noble raiment of heavenly glory; but St. Francis seemed to be dressed in a more beautiful garment than St. John." John tells the amazed friar that he and Mary have suffered the most, but right behind them, Francis "felt greater sorrow than any other" (*Flowers*: 44).

The hagiographers have no doubt that Francis entered the heavenly throng two years before his death, when the wounds appeared. From then on, he is barely human—far more a divinity than a man who learned his own psychological and spiritual potential by conducting relentless experiments. We are led to believe that Francis was so much a superior being in comparison with the rest of us that we can do nothing but admire. We certainly could not be expected to emulate him in any serious way, that is, work out a sadhana of our own and find the Yahweh of the unique and personal being that we are. This is, in fact, what truly sets Francis apart from the majority of faithful Christians. He started out with a simple but vague notion of God derived from the Bible; and in trying to serve that God, he found he had to pay attention to the only source of feedback available, his own body-and-mind. Fifteen or twenty years of experimentation with poverty and contemplation was interrupted by a shock of dissent from his friars and led him to so complex an image of God that the average individual both of his day and our own is apt to find it deeply disturbing. The similarities that God shares with the irascible God of the Old Testament and the wrathful gods of Hinduism and Buddhism, together with Francis's contention that the devils are not the opponents but the constables of God and Rudolf Otto's mysterium tremendum et fascinans: all these parallels imply that Francis's God is not merely idiosyncratic to a single countercultural figure of the thirteenth century.

His troubles, his Great Temptation, led him to a more comprehensive vision of God than his time, the Roman church, or indeed Western culture has been able to accept. In the end, then, it is not the bishop of Assisi or even Pope Gregory IX that pulled a veil over Francis. We all do when we prefer the holy simpleton who preached to the birds and convinced both the wolf of Gubbio and a band of robbers to give up their "wrathful" ways. Doubtlessly such a Francis did exist, back in the early days before the stories were composed. Such stories have been remembered because they correspond to the common view of Francis. They are as true as we can find; but they ignore the essential point, that Francis was a *conscious* mystic. He achieved what he did by paying close attention to his states of awareness and the sorts of events that influenced them.

By the time Francis had begun cultivating the self-confidence of his novices before sending them out on begging expeditions, he had already learned a great deal about the variable stability of his ego, the dangerous riches of the narcissistic region of his psyche, and a few techniques he could use to open the door to the kingdom-of-heaven perspective. Possibly he reached a stage where he could trick the devils (fool God, in effect) and steal a few hours of sleep. But a careful observer of conscious states like Francis could not long forestall the realization that the ecstatic world he visited was not simply a Mansion of Fun. It was an Earth of (Hard) Reality that he had discovered. He found a God as dangerous and capricious as a cyclone or volcano, but one who fascinated and inspired so well that Francis could do nothing but embrace that cosmos and that God.

TEN

The Throne of Lucifer

In the morning Brother Pacificus . . . was caught up in ecstasy . . . [and] saw a host of thrones in the sky; one, higher than all the others, was radiant with the glory and brilliance of all kinds of precious stones. Admiring its splendor, he wondered what this throne was and for whom it was prepared. Suddenly he heard a voice say to him: "This was Lucifer's throne. Blessed Francis will occupy it in his stead."

. . . Pretending that nothing had happened, for he did not want to reveal his vision, he asked blessed Francis: "Brother, what do you think of yourself?" "I think," he answered, "that I am the greatest of sinners." Immediately Brother Pacificus heard the voice in his heart saying to him: "By this sign you will recognize the truth of your vision: just as Lucifer was hurled from his throne because of pride, so will blessed Francis deserve to be exalted because of his humility and take his place" (*Perugia*: 23).

B Y THE TIME he had been laid out naked on the ground to die, God's Simpleton had suffered some major complications. Although

nothing seemed more straightforward than the choice of poverty, difficulties had begun at once. Giving things away brought him face to
face with narcissism. Reversing the values of the material world
required an internal reversal. What made him feel grand poisoned his
spirit, and what brought shame transfigured it. He set out to serve a
loving and generous God, the antithesis of his driven, upwardly
mobile father, but found a tormentor of body-and-mind. Francis the
Simpleton saw his body as the enemy of mystical practice, but Francis
the Stigmatic learned that the sadhana itself had become his greatest
obstacle. For although the body tends to anchor us in the profane
world through its love of comfort, anchors are everywhere. Francis
found himself anchored to his sadhana, the method of spiritual experimentation he had refined enough to render transmissible.

His Great Temptation was his tormented response to a fait
accompli: poverty as a sadhana was to be buried, while poverty as a
pious affectation would survive. It was an insult to everything he stood
for. But worse than that, it was a religious, spiritual, and political disaster; for the passageway to God he had discovered would remain a
secret; the world would not be changed; and to complete the deal,
God required his acquiescence. Was it possible God wished to remain
inaccessible or that the constabulary God had a sadistic streak? If
Francis learned anything from his two years of struggle and if the stigmata represented genuine transcendence and not a "conversion symptom" of neurotic escape, he must have realized this last test was not so
different from the ones that had gone before. For although the sadhana of poverty selected trading downward as its characteristic focus,
we have seen repeatedly that what truly counted in Francis's mystical
practice was attending to his awareness. Every move in the strategy of
poverty stirred up reactions in his body-and-mind that constituted the
real spiritual challenge. Every choice he made, every action he took,
reopened old issues and required new conquests of himself. Each
moment-by-moment battle pared down his life and left it simpler. In
the end there was nothing left but the method itself and his conviction
that it was the royal road to the kingdom of heaven as a mode of seeing and way of life.

To illustrate what this might mean for us, we can conduct a
"thought experiment" employing some of the principles we have
learned from the inner life of Francis. Imagine a contemporary man,

perhaps a computer programmer with a small family, who is convinced there has to be more to life than his contemporaries seem to assume. He happens on the story of Francis of Assisi and concludes, as we have, that the sadhana of poverty is but one form a spiritual life might take. Because trading downward would be unfair to his wife and children, he casts about for another discipline, one that will be less obvious to the outer world. Although such a plan would seem to diminish the narcissistic issue of shame in the eyes of his contemporaries that was so important in Francis's initiation, Brother Ass and the anchor of bodily comfort will still play an important role. Perhaps he notes that he has already become somewhat thick in the waist and takes it as an indication that there are some strong attachments in the area of food.

Pursuing a sadhana of fasting, however, is not the same as going on a diet. Indeed, there is something deeply conflictual in the very choice of this sadhana. For if he is successful in reducing his food intake, his ego will surely be gratified to imagine and possibly eventually to have a trim, new figure. Our programmer's narcissistic need for admiration will threaten to turn his spiritual aspirations inside out and employ them to solidify the habitual concerns of the conventional world. If there is a way out of this predicament, he will have to discover it on his own in the course of his battle with himself.

There is another drawback to the sadhana of fasting. Our spiritual experimenter will be determined not to disregard his health, lest he compromise his family responsibilities. Furthermore, Francis's early follies have shown quite clearly that the abuse of Brother Ass was a mistake. Our man's eating practices, therefore, can have nothing absolute about them—nothing as simple as Francis's finding beggars more poorly clad than himself with whom he could trade garments. The programmer will have no external measure by which to judge his progress. If he is to practice fasting while maintaining the vigorous health of his body, it will not be possible to measure each day's food ration, for instance, to ensure that it does not exceed yesterday's. For what makes an exercise a sadhana is not a rigid plan of asceticism but rather the attention it directs back upon our own awareness. No rational program of steps can be designed in advance to assure the practitioner he is on the right track. He has to navigate, rather, by attending to disturbances in his body-and-mind. He will learn to discriminate a wide array of types and degrees of hunger as well as the various ways of feeling satisfied.

What we usually associate with fasting and dieting overrides the protests of body-and-mind while perhaps seeking to induce altered states of consciousness by maintaining an empty stomach. In a *sadhana* of fasting, however, there will be no counting of calories and no favored or restricted types of food. Our would-be mystic will eat what is put before him or choose from the list of possibilities in the restaurant menu. If his dinner partners are aware of his practice, he may imitate Francis in designating one of them as his temporary "superior" to make the menu decision for him. The purpose of a sadhana is to dislodge the ego from the director's chair, to accept as much as possible what the world provides, to resemble Francis's birds of the air and lilies of the field. A sadhana of fasting, in fact, will not array itself against the body as though this lump of flesh were an enemy of spirituality. Rather it will embrace the body as a partner in the quest.

The body's hunger, satiety, and energy level will all figure in a moment's judgment about laying down the fork or asking that the carrots be passed. It is not a matter of denying oneself treats but of discerning which impulses belong to the body as its essential needs and which are passing whims that serve primarily to distract one from one's sadhana. By sharpening his consciousness of bodily and emotional states, our proto-mystic will enter a field of concern that is no longer part of the conventional world. Paying attention to his consciousness is a radical act, a withdrawal from the everyday but not yet an entry into an alternate cosmos. In the beginning his efforts will have to be devoted almost exclusively to staying in this transitional space, where dialogue between observing ego and the awareness of body-and-mind is conducted. The pure enjoyment of tasting, chewing, and swallowing always threatens to overwhelm his attention, draw it away from his sadhana, and reestablish mindless eating as the "default" state of consciousness.

If our spiritual novice is determined, patient, and returns again and again to mindful eating despite all the failures and distractions, he may find after a few months of diligence that the shift in his attention has become more easy to sustain. This will be his first real "breakthrough," the first time he can feel that his sadhana is beginning to take on a life of its own. Indeed, Francis has made it clear through his biographers that as long as we are straining with ego-directed effort we have not found the "perfect joy" that marks the path of a genuine sadhana. We know we are on that path only when we find that it is no longer we who do the work but that we are carried along by a larger current of interest—something like Francis's erotic involvement with Lady Poverty.

With this breakthrough, however, everything becomes possible. For now our attention can direct itself as readily to awareness of our body-and-mind as it can to an altercation that has just flared up in the street outside our window. Consequently, the practitioner of joyful fasting will find himself entering that transitional space of body-and-mind awareness even when he is not sitting down to eat, and even when he does not intend to do so. While driving his car, dandling his daughter, or making love to his wife, our proto-mystic will become momentarily aware of what *it* is doing, the body-and-mind which is the real agent of his life. The illusion of the ego's control is finally being undermined, and the ego-membrane thinned out. At first he will experience only flashes of this alternate perspective, perhaps once every week or two. Gradually, however, these moments will become more frequent; and as they do, the taken-for-granted nature of the conventional world will be as radically undermined as the ego. Portals to an ecstatic world may be found, and if the evidence of Francis's life does not lead us astray, we can expect encounters with the narcissistic emotions to become more frequent.

Portals to an alternate cosmos will surely emerge once the conventional world and habitual ego have been undermined. But we have imagined no shape for that world and no exercises by which our proto-mystic might assist his entry into what corresponds to Francis's kingdom of heaven. Francis employed the Bible rather aggressively in preparing his consciousness for the sacred cosmos. He repeated favorite verses, composed canticles, and above all designed for himself an intensive all-day meditation on the passion and death of Christ. Our computer programmer may not be capable of this sort of relationship with the Bible. He may have to attend to his own unconscious as it manifests in his dreams, waking fantasies, and especially those moments when the conventional world begins to break up or fade out, in order to find the mythic foundations of his own life. Perhaps, like Francis, he will devote years to composing and refining phrases to

repeat and images to contemplate. Furthermore, he might try a form
of dharma preaching, even if he has no community in which to do so.
He can, for instance, speak spontaneously of the other world, aloud,
while driving alone in his car. If he does so, he will attend to how readily the words come and whether they seem to be generated from
somewhere other than his ego.

Paralleling the story of Francis's life, our "thought experiment"
employs the Poverello's discovery that each moment of the day and
night provides an opportunity either to reassert the conventional
world-construction of our habitual ego-attitude or to open ourselves
to an unpredictable rearrangement of the world. The latter alternative
may be too frightening for most of us to consider—or even to entertain as an abstract possibility—for if we do embark on such a course,
we are in for a radical rearrangement of ourselves. Every step along
the way takes the form of an insult to our ego's pride of accomplishment and mastery. It makes no difference what practice we take up to
get us started—trading downward, eating mindfully, or something
entirely different—its essence will always come down to finding and
overturning the ever more subtle ways by which our habits reassert
themselves. The work always takes us to the narcissistic sector of our
body-and-mind where the ego stands on shaky ground. Again and
again, we have to relinquish our preconceptions and open ourselves to
reality as it is rather than what we want it to be and habitually construe
it. Every step is a letting-go of a formerly unconscious attachment and
a stepping-down from an inadvertent pretense.

This is why Brother Pacificus' vision of the Throne of Lucifer is
so apt. According to tradition, Lucifer the "Light Bearer" was once
the loftiest of the angels but had to be expelled from heaven for his
pride. He is, therefore, the model of an overconfident ego and represents the antithesis of trading downward. Every "enthroned" ego is
necessarily excluded from the ecstatic world, for ecstasy is precisely
leaving the throne and standing outside one's habitual self. Ecstasy
supervenes only when the ego has been moved out of the driver's seat
and becomes an observer of realities generated elsewhere. When
Francis vacated that seat, he found himself to be "the greatest of sinners." He was thinking of how ungrateful he was in view of all the
favors the director of his ecstasies had shown him; how easily he was
distracted and forgot to observe his awareness of body-and-mind; and

how ready he was to take up the cudgels for an idea or practice he believed in so fiercely that he had become attached to it. His sinfulness was a good deal more subtle than ours, but he was no less burdened by it. When Francis called himself a sinner, he was referring to what he had learned in his bouts with the narcissistic emotions.

The claim that Lucifer's throne has been reserved for Francis signifies not merely the glorification of the Poverello's saintly life but commends his methods as well. For his techniques of ecstasy always involved standing aside and standing down. His employment of the narcissistic emotions deliberately challenged the ego and "unseated" it so as to open the way for the wholly unanticipated to enter consciousness. In the end, the Throne of Lucifer stands for the narcissistic extremes of grandiosity and shame. Lucifer clung pig-headedly to his grandiose throne and was hurled sprawling into the shameful depths. Francis willingly chose to enter the domain of his shameful shadow, rolled in it like a pig, and thereby lighted up his body-and-mind from within. The throne belongs to him because he knows his grandiose impulses better than anyone, and how to convert them into light.

Bibliography

Allione, Tsultrim. *Women of Wisdom*. Boston: Arkana, 1986.

Armstrong, Regis J., O.F.M., Cap., and Ignatius Brady, O.F.M. (Translators and Introduction). *Francis and Clare: The Compete Works*. New York: Paulist Press, 1982.

Barks, Coleman, and John Moyne (Translators). *Open Secret: Versions of Rumi*. Putney, VT: Threshold Books, 1984.

——. *This Longing: Poetry, Teaching Stories, and Letters of Rumi*. Putney, VT: Threshold Books, 1988.

Battacharya, Brajamadhava. *The World of Tantra*. New Delhi: Munshiram Manoharlal, 1988.

Bodo, Murray, O.F.M. *The Way of St. Francis: The Challenge of Franciscan Spirituality for Everyone*. Garden City, NY: Image, 1984.

David Bohm. *Wholeness and the Implicate Order*. New York: Ark, 1983.

Bonaventure. *The Life of Saint Francis*. Translated and introduced by Ewert Cousins. New York: Paulist Press, 1978: pp. 177–328.

Cantor, Norman F. *The Civilization of the Middle Ages*. New York: HarperCollins, 1994.

Chesterton, G. K. *St. Francis of Assisi*. Garden City, NY: Image, 1957.

Cohn, Norman. *The Pursuit of the Millennium: Revolutionary Millenarians and Mystical Anarchists of the Middle Ages*. New York: Oxford, 1970.

Daniélou, Alain. *Gods of Love and Ecstasy: The Traditions of Shiva and Dionysus*. Rochester, VT: Inner Traditions International, 1992.

David-Neel, Alexandra. *Magic and Mystery in Tibet*. Baltimore: Penguin, 1971.

de Robeck, Nesta. *St. Clare of Assisi*. Chicago: Franciscan Herald Press, 1980.

Deutsch, Eliot (Translator). *The Bhagavad Gita*. New York: Holt, Rinehart, and Winston, 1968.

Eliade, Mircea. *Yoga: Immortality and Freedom*. Translated by W. R. Trask. Princeton: Princeton University Press, 1969.

Englebert, Omer. *Saint Francis of Assisi: A Biography*. Second English edition revised and augmented by Ignatius Brady, O.F.M., and Raphael Brown. Translated by Eve Marie Cooper. Ann Arbor: Servant Books, 1979.

Erikson, Joan Mowat. *Saint Francis and His Four Ladies*. New York: W. W. Norton, 1970.

Feuerstein, Georg. *Encyclopedic Dictionary of Yoga*. New York: Paragon, 1990.

Fischer-Schreiber, Ingrid, Franz-Karl Ehrhard, Kurt Friedrichs, & Michael S. Diener. *The Encyclopedia of Eastern Philosophy and Religion: Buddhism, Hinduism, Taoism, Zen*. Translated by M. H. Hohn, K. Ready, & W. Wünsche. Boston: Shambhala, 1989.

Freud, Sigmund. *The Standard Edition of the Complete Psychological Works*. Translated and edited by James Strachey, et. al., London: Hogarth, 1966.

Frugoni, Chiara. *Francis of Assisi: A Life*. Translated by John Bowden. New York: Continuum, 1998.

Glassé, Cyril. *The Concise Encyclopedia of Islam*. San Francisco: Harper & Row, 1989.

Habig, Marion A. (Ed.). *St. Francis of Assisi, Writings and Early Biographies: English Omnibus of the Sources for the Life of St. Francis*. Chicago: Franciscan Herald Press, 1983.

Hartmann, Ernest. *Boundaries in the Mind: A New Psychology of Personality*. U.S.A.: BasicBooks, 1991.

Haule, John Ryan. "From Somnambulism to the Archetypes: The French Roots of Jung's Split with Freud." *Psychoanalytic Review* 71(4) (1984): 95–107.

———. *Perils of the Soul: Ancient Wisdom and the New Age*. York, ME: Weiser, 1999.

Hershock, Peter D. *Liberating Intimacy: Enlightenment and Social Virtuosity in Ch'an Buddhism*. Albany: SUNY, 1996.

Ibn [al-] 'Arabi, Muhyiddin. *Journey to the Lord of Power: A Sufi Manual on Retreat*. Translated by Rabia Terri Harris. Rochester, VT: Inner Traditions International, 1989.

———. *Sufis of Andalusia: The* Ruh al-quds *and* al-Durrat al-fahkirah *of Ibn 'Arabi*. Translated with Introduction and Notes by R. W. J. Austin. Berkeley: University of California Press, 1971.

Janet, Pierre. *De l'angoisse a l'extase: Etudes sur les croyances at les sentiments* (1926). Two volumes, reprinted Paris: Société Pierre Janet, 1975.

———. *Les obsessions et la psychasthénie* (1903). Two volumes, reprinted, New York: Arno, 1976.

Jung, C. G. "Marriage as a Psychological Relationship" (1926). In *CW 17*: 189–210.

———. *Memories, Dreams, Reflections*. Recorded and edited by Aniela Jaffé. Translated by Richard and Clara Winston. New York: Pantheon, 1961.

———. "On Psychic Energy" (1928/48). In *CW 8*: 3–66.

———. [*CW 6*] *Psychological Types*. 1971.

———. *The Psychology of Kundalini Yoga: Notes of the Seminar Given in 1932 by C. G. Jung*. Edited by Sonu Shamdasani. Princeton: Bollingen, 1996.

———. "Synchronicity: An Acausal Connecting Principle" (1955). In *CW 8*: 417–531.

———. [*CW 7*] *Two Essays in Analytical Psychology*. 1966.

Kinsley, David. *Tantric Visions of the Divine Feminine*. Berkeley: University of California Press, 1997.

Klein, Melanie. *The Psycho-Analysis of Children*. London: Hogarth, 1932.

Kohut, Heinz. *The Analysis of the Self.* Madison, CT: Internaltional Universities Press, 1971.

——. *The Restoration of the Self.* New York: International Universities, 1977.

——. *Self Psychology and the Humanities: Reflections on a New Psychoanalytic Approach.* Edited by C. B. Strozier. New York: W. W. Norton, 1985.

Kripal, Jeffrey J. *Kali's Child: The Mystical and the Erotic in the Life and Teachings of Ramakrishna.* Chicago: University of Chicago Press, 1995.

McBrien, Richard P. *Catholicism: Study Edition.* Minneapolis: Winston Press, 1981.

McDaniel, June. *The Madness of the Saints: Ecstatic Religion in Bengal.* Chicago: University of Chicago Press, 1989.

Messiaen, Olivier. *Saint Francois d'Assise: Scènes franciscaines en trois actes et huit tableaux.* The Hallé Orchestra under Kent Nagano and the Arnold Schoenberg Choir under Erwin Ortner. Hamburg: Deutsche Grammophon, 1999.

Nikhilananda, Swami. *The Upanishads.* Abridged Edition. New York: Harper Torchbooks, 1963.

Nizami. *The Story of Layla and Majnun.* Translated and edited by R. Gelpke with E. Mattin and G. Hill. Boulder, CO: Shambhala, 1966.

Otto, Rudolf. *The Idea of the Holy.* Translated by John W. Harvey. New York: Oxford, 1917/58.

Rougemont, Denis de. *Love in the Western World.* Translated by M. Belgion. Princeton: Princeton University Press, 1956/72.

Schmucki, Octavian, O.F.M., Cap. *The Stigmata of St. Francis of Assisi: A Critical Investigation in Light of the Thirteenth-Century Sources.* Translated by Canisius F. Connors, O.F.M. St. Bonaventure, New York: The Franciscan Institute, 1991.

Scholem, Gershom G. *Major Trends in Jewish Mysticism.* New York: Schocken, 1969.

Sheldrake, Rupert. *The Presence of the Past: Morphic Resonance and the Habits of Nature.* Rochester, VT: Park Street Press, 1995.

Tuchman, Barbara W. *A Distant Mirror: The Calamitous 14th Century.* New York: Ballantine, 1978.

Underhill, Evelyn. *Mysticism: A Study in the Nature and Development of Man's Spiritual Consciousness.* New York: E. P. Dutton, 1961.

Walsh, James J. *The Thirteenth: Greatest of Centuries.* New York: Knights of Columbus, 1913.

Wilson, Peter Lamborn. *Scandal: Essays in Islamic Heresy.* New York: Autonomedia, 1988.

——. *Sacred Drift: Essays on the Margins of Islam.* San Francisco: City Lights Books, 1993.

Notes

1. "The textile industry was the automobile industry of the Middle Ages" (Tuchman, 1978: 39).
2. For abbreviations, see "A Note on the Early Biographies" immediately following the Table of Contents.
3. Norman Cantor, in his influential history of the Middle Ages, tells us that although monks were to live a life of constant prayer supported by their own labor, by 800 most monasteries were supported by the labor of serfs, and the monks themselves were almost exclusively drawn from the nobility. "By the tenth century, the black monks [Benedictines] owned a considerable part of the best farmland in Western Europe . . . [and] were required to become vassals of the king or duke and to send knights to the armies of their lords." They became scholars, bishops, popes, and advisors and administrators of kings (Cantor, 1994: 154).
4. The twelfth century Muslim mystic, Ibn al-'Arabi gives many such example from his life according to R.W.J. Austin (Translator and Editor), *Sufis of Andalusia: The* Ruh al-quds *and* al-Durrat al-fakhirah *of Ibn 'Arabi*. Los Angeles: University of California Press, 1977.
5. E.g., Thomas Sugrue, *There is a River: The Story of Edgar Cayce*. Virginia Beach: A.R.E. Press, 1994.
6. By sheer coincidence, Shiva's consort's name, Parvati (PAR-vuh-tee), even sounds like Poverty.
7. In "Admonition II" to his friars, Francis says, "For the person eats of the tree of knowledge of good and evil who appropriates to himself his own will and thus exults himself over the good things which the Lord says and does in him" (Armstrong & Brady, 1982: 27).
8. Regarding the link between intoxication and speaking a "second language," I have noted that I do much better in my second language after I have had a glass of wine.
9. Francis expressed the lesson he learned from this experiment in "Admonition XVII": "Blessed is that servant who does not pride himself on the good that

179

the Lord says or does through him any more than on what He says or does through another" (Armstrong & Brady, 1982: 32f).

10. Cf. the work of Heinz Kohut, e.g. Kohut (1977).

11. Francis recommended this sentiment to his friars in "Admonition V": "All the creatures under heaven, each according to his nature, serve, know, and obey their Creator better than you" (Armstrong & Brady, 1982: 29).

12. Bonaventure's *MinLife* was written as an addition to the Divine Office, which is sometimes called the "Prayer of the Church." Every Roman Catholic priest is obliged to recite it every day.

13. A common Buddhist expression.

14. According to the biographies, Francis called himself *il poverello*, "the little poor man."

15. The original Latin title is *Sacrum Commercium Sancti Francisci cum Domina Paupertate*, which might be translated as "The Sacred Commerce of St. Francis with Lady Poverty" except that *commerce* is a peculiar English word in this context. The translator, Placid Hermann, O.F.M., points out that the Latin phrase, *habere commercium* (literally, "to have commerce"), may be translated as "to dwell with familiarly" (Habig, 1983: 1537). In his "Introduction," he tells us he prefers the title, "The Sacred Romance of St. Francis with Lady Poverty" (*Ibid.*, 1533, n. 8); but the translated work nevertheless appears as *Sacrum Commercium or Francis and His Lady Poverty*. Evidently the title was too hot to handle. Noting that the English word *commerce* may sometimes refer to sexual dealings, that one of the meanings of *commercium* is "intercourse" (Cassell's Latin-English Dictionary), and furthermore that *intercourse* is a word not limited to the sexual domain, though it strongly suggests it, I prefer to translate the title as *The Holy Intercourse of St. Francis with Lady Poverty*.

16. The painting is sometimes said to be the work of Giotto, who did many of the Assisi murals.

17. Today it is thought Francis suffered from an infection of the cornea (trachoma) perhaps caught while in the Middle East. This would account for his painful sensitivity to light, and excessive tearing. His doctors advised him to resist the "gift of tears," whereby he wept for the sufferings of Christ, because they thought excessive lacrimation was injuring his sight. Francis is said to have refused, valuing the sacred world of his biblically inspired weeping over the everyday of profane sight. In light of modern medical knowledge, it appears that his "gift of tears" was the symptom of his disease and not its cause. This is, however, not to deny the "gift of tears" as a possible manifestation of religious ecstasy; for notable saints, such as Ignatius of Loyola (Catholic) and Ibn al-'Arabi (Muslim) apparently had the gift without the deleterious effects of trachoma. The gift of tears may also be related to the Hindu god, Shiva; for "Shiva" ("the Benevolent") is apparently a euphemistic variant name for the older god, Rudra, whose name means "He who causes tears" (Daniélou, 1992: 49).

18. Here is a possible borrowing from the Islamic tradition, where the *hadith* (oral-tradition reports of the actions and words of Muhammad) are always backed up by an *isnad*, or chain of dependable transmissions.

19. De Robeck cites Thomas of Celano as the source of this quotation.

20. A *dakini*, a female wisdom principle of boundless spontaneity.
21. Often the saints of Hinduism and Buddhism are provided with previous lives of extraordinary achievement by way of accounting for spectacular attainments in this life. They seem to have had a huge head start over the rest of us. For example, in her life just before being born as Machig Lapdron, the religious heroine was a man who had received his initiation on the mystical path from a woman.
22. Rumi was born in present-day Afghanistan fifteen years later than Francis.
23. Although this incident comes from only the third anecdote of *Flowers*, the author begins by saying that Francis was blind from his constant weeping, which would mean that it comes from late in the Poverello's life. I believe this chronologically inconsistent detail was added to explain how it was that Francis could call himself a "blind man." I prefer to think that Francis was describing himself as *spiritually* blind, for this alone would make sense of the anecdote.
24. "Hamlet of the Holy Sepulcher," i.e., named after the place where Christ was buried, and also the place where Francis is so ecstatic he resembles a corpse. The symbolic correspondences of the biographies are marvelous. Nevertheless, there is a town named Borgo San Sepolcro right about where the biography says it is, about twenty-two miles northeast of Arezzo.
25. Schmucki quotes a medieval "liturgical legend" that says: Francis "used the same tunic day and night for his clothing and his bed. The tunic was covered with worms but was made more bearable by frequent shaking." Schmucki comments, "Presupposing the historical truth of this new element, we have to consider that they were fleas rather than worms" (Schmucki, 1991: 241, n. 55).
26. R. M. French (Translator), *The Way of a Pilgrim* and *The Pilgrim Continues His Way*. San Francisco, Harper SanFrancisco, 1973.
27. This felicitous translation by Gary Wills appeared in the *National Catholic Reporter*, March 16, 1966.
28. Cf. *1Celano*: 26-28; *2Celano*: 27, 30.
29. Cf. *2Celano*: 31; *3Celano*: 41.
30. Cf. *MajLife*: IV, 4; *1Celano*: 48.
31. Cf. *1Celano*: 69-72; *2Celano*: 115, 122; *Perugia*: 23.
32. Cf. *1Celano*: 61-67; *3Celano*: 17.
33. Cf. *1Celano*: 58, 61; *2Celano*: 165, 166, 171.
34. Ibn al-'Arabi was born in Spain in 1165, just seventeen years before Francis was born in Italy.
35. "It is wise not to identify with these experiences, but to handle them as if they were outside the human realm. That is the safest thing to do—and really absolutely necessary. Otherwise you get an inflation, and inflation is just a minor form of lunacy, a mitigated term for it. And if you get so absolutely inflated that you burst, it is schizophrenia" (Jung, 1996: 27).
36. DSM-IV, pp. 658–61: *Diagnostic and Statistical Manual of Mental Disorders, Fourth Edition*. Washington, D.C.: American Psychiatric Association, 1994.
37. I have discussed clairvoyance at some length in *Perils of the Soul* (Haule, 1999: 43–56).

38. For example, Milton H. Erickson, "The Hypnotic Alteration of Blood Flow: An Experiment Comparing Waking and Hypnotic Responsiveness." In E. L. Rossi (Ed.), *The Collected Papers of Milton H. Erickson on Hypnosis*, Vol. II, New York: Irvington, 1980: 192–5.

39. Quoting the *Shatapatha-Brahmana*.

40. Thomas of Spalato says he was a student when he joined a throng in the Bologna marketplace to hear Francis preach (de Robeck, 1980: 30).

41. Celano and the other biographers wish to emphasize the solidity of Francis's celibacy in reminding us that he rarely visited Clare. Today we might suspect him of being a bit obsessed. As we shall see, the reason he hated to go there may have been the high expectations of the nuns.

42. The Psalm in question is counted as #50 by Catholics and #51 by Protestants. In the Challoner-Douay Catholic translation of the Bible, the psalm begins: "For the leader. A psalm of David, when Nathan the prophet came to him after his sin with Bethsabee. Have mercy on me, O God, in your goodness; in the greatness of your compassion wipe out my offense."

43. In justification of my free "translations" of *dharma*, a Sanskrit term with many meanings, I would point out that *dharma* is used to mean truth, reality, or fact; duty, custom, or how things are to be done; and also the eternal substance of the Buddha, his "*dharma* body." Nothing is more "sublime and transcending" than that. The Buddha's *dharma* body corresponds to the eternal Christ, his *historical* body as Gautama Shakyamuni corresponds to Jesus of Nazareth, and the Buddha's "*enjoyment* body" to the apparitional post-resurrection Christ.

44. Lin-chi I-hsüan, known in Japanese as Rinzai Gigen, d. 866/7. Founder of a school named after himself which became the most influential school of Ch'an and the most vital school of Chinese Buddhism (Fischer-Schreiber, *et. al.*, 1989).

45. "The most loved masters of Ch'an . . . are those who display the wildest personas, whose teaching is the most iconoclastic. . . . [E]ach one of them is what we might call a "real character," a kind of spiritual maverick. Some are outright rascals . . ." (Hershock, 1996: 191).

46. Thomas of Spalato (Erickson, 1970: 126) and Roger of Wendover (Frugoni, 1998: 79) both provide versions of this tale.

47. For this distinction between *trance* and *reverie* I am indebted to Dan Merkur, *Becoming Half Hidden: Shamanism and Initiation Among the Inuit*. New York: Garland, 1992, pp. 68–84. Merkur says that trance is characterized by "involuntary belief," the entranced individual has no choice but to accept the reality of the vision as simply what is. Such "involuntary belief" is what I mean to imply by the notion that the sacred cosmos may sometimes overwhelm and obliterate the conventional world and seem to be the only universe there is.

48. The paragraphs are not numbered in Part II of *Flowers*. Here, the passage appears in Habig, 1983: 1483).

49. E.g., John 7:37.

50. 1 Corinthians 10:4.

51. This last sentiment is one that brings Francis close to the sensitivity to words and letters and their symbolic significance that was deeply explored by the

Jewish Cabalists of Spain from the twelfth to fifteenth centuries (cf. Scholem, 1969).

52. Cf. Quran 25:55; 55:20; 23:100.

53. "The high priest of the Roman State was called the *Pontifex Maximus* [the greatest bridge-builder], a title assumed eventually by the pope and only recently disavowed by Popes John Paul I (d. 1978) and John Paul II" (McBrien, 1981: 259).

54. For example, bands of "spirituals" set out for Jerusalem nearly every decade, proving their faithfulness to the "Spirit" by killing Jews, Muslims, aristocrats, or priests, depending on their theology, refusing to work, and stealing and killing when begging did not suffice (Cohn, 1970).

55. Often spelled Hugolino or Ugolino, named Pope Gregory IX a little over a year after Francis's death—an honor that is said to have been predicted by Francis. He is the one who suppressed the "Testament" by which Francis hoped to remind the friars of his mystical roots and their own.

56. Leo's failure to grasp the essence of Francis's message has been made famous by his embrace of the larger church's vision for the Franciscan Order: namely his extravagant building program.

57. The feast existed in the thirteenth century, although the mythic event was not proclaimed a "dogma" of the Roman church until 1950 by Pius XII.

58. Schmucki reports a female Bulgarian Orthodox in the eighteenth or nineteenth century and a member of the ancient, heretical Monophysite Church in 1940—both of them mystically-inclined Christian churches (Schmucki, 1991: 44).